THE TRUTH ABOUT STYLE

THE TRUTH ABOUT STYLE

Stacy London

VIKING

VIKING
Published by the Penguin Group
Penguin Group (USA) Inc., 375 Hudson Street, New York, New York 10014, U.S.A.
Penguin Group (Canada), 90 Eglinton Avenue East, Suite 700, Toronto,
Ontario, Canada M4P 2Y3 (a division of Pearson Penguin Canada Inc.)
Penguin Books Ltd, 80 Strand, London WC2R 0RL, England
Penguin Ireland, 25 St. Stephen's Green, Dublin 2, Ireland (a division of Penguin Books Ltd)
Penguin Books Australia Ltd, 250 Camberwell Road, Camberwell, Victoria 3124,
Australia (a division of Pearson Australia Group Pty Ltd)
Penguin Books India Pvt Ltd, 11 Community Centre, Panchsheel Park, New Delhi – 110 017, India
Penguin Group (NZ), 67 Apollo Drive, Rosedale, Auckland 0632,
New Zealand (a division of Pearson New Zealand Ltd)
Penguin Books (South Africa) (Pty) Ltd, 24 Sturdee Avenue,
Rosebank, Johannesburg 2196, South Africa

Penguin Books Ltd, Registered Offices: 80 Strand, London WC2R 0RL, England

First published in 2012 by Viking Penguin, a member of Penguin Group (USA) Inc.

1   3   5   7   9   10   8   6   4   2

PHOTOGRAPH CREDITS
All photos are the property of Furry Purry, Inc. with the exception of the following:
Courtesy of Stacy London: Pages 11, 12, 14, 15, 19, 22, 33
Courtesy of Vicki London: Page 34

LIBRARY OF CONGRESS CATALOGING IN PUBLICATION DATA
London, Stacy.
The truth about style / Stacy London.
p. cm.
ISBN 978-0-670-02623-4 (hardback)
1. Fashion--Psychological aspects. 2. Personality. 3. Self-esteem. 4. Expression (Philosophy) I. Title.
TT507.L73 2012   746.9'2--dc23   2012015144

Printed in the United States of America
Set in Bauer Bodoni Std, Bodoni Std, and Neutraface Text
Designed by Renato Stanisic

ALWAYS LEARNING   PEARSON

To snowflakes everywhere:
What can I say? I'm a cheeseball when it comes to this stuff.

To all my haters:
You made me the smart bitch I am today. Mwah.

To Mary:
This one's for you, Grandma.

"I think that young men and women are so caught by the way they see themselves. Now mind you, when a larger society sees them as unattractive, as threats, as too black or too white or too poor or too fat or too thin or too sexual or too asexual, that's rough. But you can overcome that. The real difficulty is to overcome how you think about yourself."

—MAYA ANGELOU

What This Book Is Not

This title is a funny one for me. If this chapter were a person, I'd never let them get away with defining themselves in the negative. But in this case, I want to dispel you of any preconceived notions you may have about this "type" of book.

Why write a book about fashion? I've struggled with this. It's not that I don't love the subject, but what else is there to say that every fashion blogger, mommy blogger, stylist, ex-model, and even I haven't already said? I mean, there are a kajillion fashion books out there already. Does anyone really need another tome to tell her what 99 items to buy, how to dress like the women on TV shows, how to dress for the red carpet, or wear shimmer? I'm not knocking "how to" books—they are often great, and necessary. But I did one of those already. My first book, *Dress Your Best*, which I coauthored, was about how to dress according to body type, just like a Colorforms manual. Why write another one? Save the trees! Keep your money! Who *needs* another fashion book?

And then I had a bit of an a-ha moment. It came to me at the home of my dear friends Molly and David, whose three children were all under the age of six at the time. These kids were like aliens—so polite, so well behaved, but inquisitive and joyous, and just such a pleasure that I had to ask Molly and David how they managed to be such wonderful parents. What was the trick? It was Zion, their son, who gave me the answer: their house rule was "Yes! . . . And?"

I sat there blankly looking at this five-year-old, waiting for him to finish the sentence. David stepped in to explain that this was the first rule of improv: The idea is to take what life has given to you, accept it wholly, and then build on that. Accept and create, essentially. Molly and David's kids had been taught to accept rules, to be creative, and their demeanor reflected what they'd been taught. It's not only a great parenting strategy but a fundamentally useful life philosophy. And as I sat there, I thought, *That's a great style philosophy, too—and one I can write a book about.*

First, consider the principle "accept what you've been given"—the "yes" part of the equation. "Yes," where style is concerned, is an unbiased, dispassionate acceptance of who you are, where your body is right now (today, not next week, after a crash diet), and what your life circumstances are. You must accept the good, the bad, and the ugly, without prejudice. "Notice, don't judge," as my sister Jaclyn once told me (attribution, sister, see?). You must get to a Zen place about the raw material you have to work with, to be able to say, "I love my back, hate my ass, I'm old, I have limited resources, and that's okay." Acceptance means knowing when your pants are too tight. It means not wearing your favorite dress when the armholes squish your chest into your armpits. When I say "accept," I mean *accept*: No more judgment, just pure dispassionate observation. The "yes" is absolutely essential to style. If you deny the reality of your body or your life, you'll never be able to dress any of it well—even the parts you love. You have to see it *all* to work with any of it.

Ignoring a problem (or a "problem area")

doesn't solve it. Trust me when I say I've tried that route many, many times. The only way to deal with a style problem is to confront it and attack it head-on. This is the "and" part of the equation, the best part of it. "Yes" is acceptance; "and" is advancing to the next step. "And" is coming up with a passionate strategy to emphasize what you love about yourself and to de-emphasize what you don't. Don't ignore your least favorite areas or try to hide them. Hiding implies a shame about ourselves. Even when you don't like something, you can accept it and "consciously camouflage" (trademark pending) it instead. Go up a size or three to look great in your pants. Strategize your spending budget. Part of "and" is using style as a tool to help create the image you want to put out in the world that tells others how you want to be treated. It can also help you foster self-esteem you didn't know you could have.

Going through the mental process of "Yes . . . and" is paramount before you try on a single article of clothing. Style doesn't start with your body—it starts with your *brain*. There has been much discussion in the last few years about neuroplasticity, the notion that the brain can reconfigure itself and form new pathways throughout life. The same can be said for how you think of your physical appearance, especially how you dress—call it the neuroplasticity of style.

For fashion-book clichés like "the

must-have trench for spring" or "three ways to rock a poncho," you'll have to go somewhere else. Let's be honest: If "how to" advice were that useful, you'd all be dressing well and I'd be out of a job. The "how to" approach is about changing your look. From years of working with women, I've discovered that that is only part of what they're really after. For that reason, my book doesn't only deal with how to dress well, and why you should, but it examines why you *don't*. We all put obstacles in our own path toward personal style, myself included. If we understood why we constructed these practical and emotional obstacles, we might move beyond them to healthier, happier perceptions of ourselves and, ideally, a better sense of self-esteem. Style can change your look, certainly, but it can also change your *life*.

And that, my dears, is What This Book *Is*.

The book is called *The Truth About Style*. But when I think about it, there's more than one truth. Or maybe there are lots of little truths that add up to one big one.

Truth: Style Is Not Fashion

Karl Lagerfeld once said, "Fashion is ephemeral, dangerous and unfair." Yikes. Fashion is also an industry. Industries are meant to make money. Fashion makes money by churning out trends that we scramble to keep up with. The images associated with it usually portray an unrealistic, unattainable beauty. The fact is, there is only one body ideal in fashion, and most likely, you don't have it. (I guess that's the unfair part Karl was talking about.) The fashion industry keeps us on a roller coaster of expectation and disappointment. It's built on, and thrives on, our collective insecurity. If style is "Yes . . . and," fashion is "No . . . but."

As in "*No*, you can't pull off or afford the dress Giselle wore on the red carpet, *but* you can buy the lipstick instead."

I'm sure someone will bash the crap out of me for saying all this (but the title isn't *The Sugarcoated Truth About Style*, now, is it?). One of the reasons the fashion business continues to succeed is that we are hardwired to judge people based on appearance. Prehistorically, that trait was useful to determine who was healthy enough to be a good mate. Being fit meant you could run away from a saber-toothed tiger long enough to procreate. A straight nose indicated better health than a crooked one (I'm out of luck there . . .), so straight noses became desirable. Today, fashion relies on our being judgmental in this way, on sizing people up. But now it's a matter not only of noses but also of which jeans we do or don't wear or what bag we will or won't carry. Obsession with looks and acquisitions draws some people in. Others find it so superficial that they opt out and ignore it completely.

Even if I could change the fashion industry, I wouldn't want to. It promotes creativity, insisting on new innovation every six months. Few industries achieve the same results so amazingly, year after year. I love the fact that styles change every season, because there is always something new to try. I realize the ever-changing variety can be hard to keep up with. But it's up to us to use the changeable nature of fashion to our advantage. And that's where style comes in.

Style, unlike fashion, is *personal*. It's about the individual. You have to know yourself in order to utilize style. Style isn't selling you a false promise.

It's reality based, and operates on the knowledge of what is right for *you*. Trust me when I say that it is always better to wear what works, what feels organic to you, than to force yourself into a current trend that simply feels wrong. Dress for yourself and what suits your lifestyle, and you will always look good.

Style is about enhancing who you are, and not attempting to look like someone you'll never be. With style, there are as many ways a woman can look beautiful as there are women. Style is yours to own and a celebration of the individual that you are. Style can make you feel empowered, stronger, and cooler. (Whatever the adjective you're after, insert it here.) Style thrives when you do. It succeeds when you are the best version of yourself, not a poor version of someone else's ideal.

It seems only right to contrast Karl Lagerfeld's quote with a Yves Saint Laurent one (they were always competing): "Over the years I have learned that what is important in a dress is the woman who is wearing it."

Truth: Style Ends with an E

What? Style does end with an E. You might think it's for Ecstasy. But it's for Emotion. Let me explain what I mean.

Lots of people say they don't know how

to dress themselves. That's an interesting conundrum, and a confounding one. As human beings, we're amazing creatures, natural problem solvers who are adapted especially well to *learning*. So what prevents us from this? The usual culprit is fear, in many forms—of the unknown, of putting oneself out there, of being judged. Such negative thoughts often become so loud that they drown the fun out of our natural curiosity.

Making excuses and letting fear rule our style stop us from expressing our true selves and what we could look like at our best. We get in the way of our own potential instead of reveling in it.

Negative thought-loops are self-perpetuating. If we don't like what we see in the mirror, we either ignore it or overcompensate for it. This causes a disconnect between who we are (smart, sophisticated, beautiful, and wonderful) and how we appear (bland, sloppy, miserable). Consciously or subconsciously, there's a disconnect when women are not dressing for—and by for I mean *really for*—themselves, like cheerleaders, all rah rah. Joy is just harder to attain.

By changing your style, you're forced to change the way you perceive yourself. And if you can see yourself differently, you can start to *feel* differently. If you put on clothes that actually flatter your figure, you suddenly may not feel as badly about your body anymore. And when the negative body feelings change—the negative *thoughts* change. When you can think positively about one aspect of yourself, it becomes easier to believe in yourself in lots of different contexts. Seeing to feeling to thinking to believing: These are the four stages of changing your style. The saying is "seeing is believing" for a reason: It's shorter.

But seriously, if you change what you see, you begin to perceive yourself differently.

Style can be as strong a motivator as a diet, exercise, and love to implement positive change in your whole life, not only the way you look. But you have to allow that to happen. Which is not as easy as that sentence makes it sound.

Truth: A Style Rut Is a Symptom

Symptoms are clues: They help doctors diagnose an underlying illness. To cure the symptoms, you have to treat the cause. Otherwise, the "cure" is only temporary and superficial.

The same is true of style. When you tell a woman who wears too much

black to change to an animal print, it's like putting a Band-Aid on a bullet hole. Coaxing her into a new top isn't ultimately going to do much for her. But asking her "Why do you wear so much black?" opens a dialogue that will take you to a core issue. (Someone once told me that if you keep asking "Why?" you will eventually get to a real answer.)

There are a million examples of how bad style can be symptomatic of an underlying problem. Baggy clothes can indicate body image issues sometimes. A bulky sweater can be a security blanket. Wearing all black or "comfortable" sweats can enable you to hide in plain sight. Overly sexy clothes can telegraph insecurity about what else the wearer has to offer, or her fear of aging, or a hunger for acceptance.

It might make you "comfortable" to ignore your appearance, but the uncomfortable truth is that appearances *do* matter. Refusing to acknowledge that how you dress sends a message to other people is a major blind spot. Our clothes, like it or not, give other people insight into who we are. To take control of the message, you have to know yourself, and dress accordingly. (Style is the quickest shorthand to who you are.)

Truth: Style Is a Choice

You have to choose to use it. Whether style is a friend or foe, a tool or an obstacle, is up to you. Style—real, true, honest-to-God organic style— can help in addressing some of the mind-sets that hold us back. It's not the only way, certainly, and it may not be the most important way. But after watching people transform through style over the years, after charting my own stylistic and emotional evolution, I am certain that it is an approach that does work. Taking control of one's image is a relatively easy method when life is uncertain, unstable, and hard. There are so many things in life that you can't control—why not take advantage of the ones you can? Style matters, peeps. Use it or lose it.

If you can get into the habit of paying attention to your own image, you can begin to work with it instead of against it by ignoring it or rejecting its importance. You can't fix what you don't allow yourself to see. Identify the problems and you are halfway there. Ignore them and you are halfway to nowhere. Consistently feeling good can help motivate you to keep on track with style. You can pay attention to the "how to" information if there is positive emotional reinforcement behind it. Caring about fashion can be vanity. Caring about style can be an opportunity.

Truth: Style Is Not a Privilege, It's a Right

People think style is a privilege of the thin, young, and rich, or at least of six-foot, one-hundred-pound fourteen-year-old Eastern European models. The truth is, it's everyone's right to feel good regardless of age, size, or budget. In whatever terms you think about yourself—good or bad—style is still yours for the taking.

We all crave affirmation from others, and the external confirmation that we are good—or even just good enough. But self-esteem ultimately has to be internally generated. If you depend completely on others for a sense of self-worth, you're not just greedy, you're needy. Style can help foster self-esteem and in turn the kind of confidence that attracts friends, lovers, employers, and coworkers into your life. Celebrate every day the person you are, and garner the level of respect you deserve.

Ignoring style is also your right, but there are plenty of compelling reasons why you shouldn't. (Quick story: When I was in tenth grade, I was failing trigonometry. Though I had tutors, I just couldn't get it, and frankly didn't much care about getting it. But my father told me something I will never forget. "If you fail out of high school, you'll be closing the door on an opportunity in the future. You limit your options every time you don't try your best," he said. If I didn't pay attention to doing my best, even when it was hard, I wouldn't have the opportunity to pick and choose what I wanted to do next, like attend the college of my choice. That advice really stuck with me—trigonometry, alas, did not.) Style is about creating possibility. It's taking passionate, strategic control of your image—not just to dress for a job you may not even have known you were going to want but for oodles of other things you can't predict for your future.

It's your right to put style in perspective, too. For everything I insist about why style matters, there are a kajillion and forty-seven reasons it doesn't. It's not as important as a friend you love and trust, or your family or doing what you love. How to prioritize style is in fact a common dilemma for modern women. Your appearance isn't the only thing you'll be judged by (I'm not *that* superficial), and your deeds and words will always matter. But style is a large part of what we see in the mirror and how we feel about ourselves. Let me be clear: Everyone deserves to dress well and feel damn good about it.

I used to think of myself as a fashion translator—someone who took high-fashion trends and turned them into digestible, wearable clothes for everyone. These days, in addition, I've started to think of myself as an interpreter, which may sound the same, but for me has a distinct difference. I can look at what you are wearing, listen to what you are saying, and find the disconnect between them. What is keeping you from applying the "how to" that you've probably heard a thousand times before?

The best way to demonstrate this is by looking at *lots* of peeps with style disconnects, to let them air their negative thoughts and struggles, and then beat the crap out of them (the negative thoughts, not the women themselves. I'm not writing *Fight Club*). I don't just want to dress the person. I want to *address* the person, as Donna Karan once said (and she's so cool). It's taken me a long time to do this for myself—a process with which I'm constantly engaged, which is why I'm in the book as well. But rather than prattle on about myself for ten chapters, I enlisted some help.

So I took to the social media that is Facebook and Twitter and asked women to send me their stories. Among the hundreds of submissions, I chose nine women to feature because I feel that their stories, though unique, are also universal. Personally, these stories resonated with me and reflected issues I could relate to in one way or another.

I invited the women to New York for a Start-over. Each woman is the sum total of her life experiences, and that never changes, but to paraphrase a Buddhist aphorism, with each breath, you have another chance to do things differently. That holds for style as well: You get another chance to start again every day, so I'm calling them Start-overs and not makeovers. These nine wanted to gain insight into their style, understand what that means to them, and imagine all the possibilities that it could bring to them in the future.

The "process" was pretty simple. The women arrived at the studio very early in the morning wearing outfits that they'd wear on a typical day (which, by the way, regardless of age or size, were almost all identical). They each sat for a portrait so that we'd have a record of their look at the "start." Next, I settled in with each woman for a chat about her style dilemma and what she hoped to get from the experience. After that, we moved into the staging area among racks of clothing, shoes, and accessories—selected by me in advance with each woman's body and lifestyle needs in mind. We tried on dozens of outfits, and talked more about each of their motivations. Together, we decided on a final look. Then each woman went into the studio for her Start-over portrait.

What happened in between is what you'll find on the following pages.

Style is a way to play with possibility. It's not the only way, but it's the one I know something about. Here's the deal: If this book offers you any insight into the way you treat and view yourself, then you can see how style can do its true job. It's not just about looking and feeling good. It's about seeing how the path to getting there is always available to you. I've learned that we can't see our blind spots until we learn a new way to see. This book is many books in one. It is about why style matters. It is about these beautiful women and the way they see themselves. And it is very much about me. So I say this to you as much as I say this to myself: Stop fighting reality. Accept what's yours. Get out of your own way and sparkle like crazy instead.

PRODUCT WARNING

If this book were a medication with a label, it would read something like this:

Side Effects Include but Are Not Limited to
renewed sense of self-esteem
increased motivation in all areas of life
You may also lose weight, fall in love, leave a bad marriage, create a better one, have closer relationships with your family, or find the job of your dreams.

Some Users Have Experienced
a kick in their step
a swing in their hips
a twinkle in their eye
Hair-tossing (commercial-style) is common, but seek medical attention if you pinch a nerve or can't stop doing it.

"Only the wounded physician heals."

—CARL JUNG

From the New York Times, *circa 1974:*
Verbose, even at age five.

Matchy-match #2, age five

Matchy-match #1, age two

Learning to Shed My Skin

It's an understatement to say that I was a fashion drama queen as a child. Anything bright, sparkly, and loud summed up my style. Before I consciously knew what it meant, I was always about making a statement. I could rest my laurels as a fashion expert on my childhood wardrobe alone really.

From the age of two I insisted on a lot of purple, and only dressed in complete outfits. (Everyone's guilty of matchy-match at least once in their life . . . okay, twice.)

When I was four I begged my mom to let me take ballet classes . . . only to walk out the first day when I found out you had to wear a leotard for rehearsals and only got to wear a tutu for recitals. No tutu every day? Bye-bye ballet.

When I was five my career ambition was to be a cocktail waitress, because it was the only job I knew of that would let me wear fishnet stockings every day. (This was before I knew there were other job options like stripper and hooker). That year for Halloween I was a sparkly flapper, in a silver dress with white fringe, a dozen rainbow bangles, and a gauzy blue headscarf. So revolutionary for its time and my age!

In kindergarten I wore party dresses and patent leather Mary Janes every day. The prettiest girl in my class, Kelly, had long red hair and stunning green eyes. I was in awe of her. On the last day of school we did a big Hawaiian-themed show for the parents. My plastic grass skirt was green, and Kelly's was pink. I spent the entire time we were waiting backstage unsuccessfully trying to convince her that pink was all wrong for her and that she should trade skirts with me. I desperately wanted the pink skirt. And I would have looked better in pink. (In retrospect, I realize it really was a good call and that I wasn't being *entirely* selfish: What redhead doesn't look good in green?)

Revolutionary for my time: twenties flapper, age five or six

Halloween, with a peach silk nightgown and matching bed jacket with a marabou collar and cuffs. For the years between flapper and madam, I was Dorothy every Halloween, because my mom had found these awesome silver slippers that she "painted" with a red Sharpie. I loved wearing my ruby slippers, though I could have taken or left the gingham dress. It was all about the shoes even then. I loved *fancy*. I loved the drama of dressing up.

I think this explains my affinity for the fashion industry. Everything is "genius." It's "heaven," and "fierce." You're in or you're out. It's all enthusiasm

When I was six, my grandmother Mary made beautiful floral-patterned housecoats for Saks Fifth Avenue. They were collarless and had snaps that went straight down the front with two huge square-patch pockets on either side. I went to my grandmother's studio one day, and she let me pick out all my favorite prints. She made me a special housecoat covered with pockets made from the different materials so I could carry all my stuffed animals with me wherever I went. It was bulky, but I wasn't concerned with body proportion in those days.

When I was eight, I was really into knit halter tops and bare midriffs and high-waisted polyester grandpa pants. If I wore shorts, they had to have rainbow satin trim. At ten I went as a madam for

Nice pants, age eight

See? Total drama queen, age ten

and drama, and always over the top. Amazeballs! Awesomesauce! I've never met a superlative I didn't like. (That's why exclamation points are my favorite punctuation mark.)

While I like to think of superlatives as expressions of unbridled enthusiasm, there are those who've pointed out that exaggeration and melodrama are forms of overcompensation for the mundane and painful. While part of me bristles at the idea that enthusiasm compensates for anything, I have to wonder if there's some truth to the theory.

I remember sitting on the powder blue carpet in the living room of our apartment listening to the Beatles' *Let It Be* when I was four. I suddenly felt an itch, a real *itch*, and when I began to scratch behind my right ear I found bumps—numerous tiny, raised pinhead-size dots. It felt like Braille had replaced my regular skin. After spending fifteen minutes trying to rub them off, I showed them to my mom.

"What's wrong with you?" she asked.

What *was* wrong with me? Trips to the dermatologist provided a diagnosis: mild psoriasis. I was prescribed a coal tar ointment to apply every night. The psoriasis was under control but didn't go away. It cropped up behind my left ear, too, and then in a little patch on my scalp.

No one could look at me and have any idea that there was something "wrong." But *I* knew there was, and the feeling that I associated with psoriasis—*something is wrong with me*—didn't go away, either. That made me feel different. Psoriasis is a permanent condition. Four was a young age to be told that you have a "permanent condition," and I didn't know anyone else who'd been given that kind of diagnosis. As a result, I never felt entirely connected to regular people. They had regular skin, and I didn't.

It was during this time that my preoccupation with clothing grew. My taste ran toward the gaudy. I wasn't trying to blend in, by any stretch. But I found comfort in the costumey and the sparkly. Much like turkeys and raccoons, I was attracted to anything shiny. I longed to be Cinderella, Snow White, and Glinda the Good Witch. All the heroines of my youth wore tiaras and sparkles. Well, Dorothy had the *shoes*. That's what I wanted.

Flash-forward seven years. I was eleven and about to start sixth grade. Early one morning, while lying under the covers of my bed in our apartment, I was awakened by a prickly, itchy, burning sensation. I looked at the Shaun Cassidy poster tacked to the ceiling above my bed and for once didn't swoon. As I tried to sort out what this weird feeling was, the burning intensified. I threw back the covers, pulled off my pajamas, and looked at my body.

My torso was covered in angry splotches. I got up and once again showed my mom.

She looked at the rash and said, "It's probably an allergic reaction to that sweater." The day before, I had worn the softest pearl-white angora sweater, which made me feel just like a bunny. I remembered then that when I had taken it off—reluctantly—to put on my PJs, I may have noticed a little redness. I didn't link the rash with the Braille behind my ear; these splotches were much angrier, much redder, and much bigger.

At first we had no idea what I had or whether it was infectious. We went to different doctors, none of whom connected the dots (no pun intended). A number of crazy diagnoses were proposed, ranging from a food allergy to some kind of cancer. Everyone had an opinion, but no one had an answer. Finally we got an appointment with a renowned dermatologist. After taking into account my whole history, including the fact that I'd had strep throat something like eighteen times the previous year, he determined that my psoriasis had progressed from mild to severe. Who knew that strep throat could advance a skin disorder? Meanwhile, during the two weeks that we visited doctors' offices, the blotches got worse, and multiplied. What had started on my torso was now rapidly covering my body from the neck down. The splotches were itchy and so dry that some of them would crack and bleed. My doctor prescribed a daily dose of penicillin, which I took for two years. I remember feeling so anxious that not only was I getting worse, but no one knew how to make me better.

For those of you who don't know what psoriasis is, it's an autoimmune disorder in which skin cells produce skin too rapidly. It gets crusty, and plaques develop. You can genetically inherit a predisposition *to* the disease but not necessarily the disease itself, which is brought on by anxiety and stress. (That tells you something about me at age four.) While it's not a life-threatening condition, ask anyone who's suffered from it and you'll discover that it involves far more than mere physical discomfort. It's a disease that's at best annoying and at worst emotionally crippling.

At eleven, I was unfamiliar with *The Metamorphosis,* Franz Kafka's novella, in which a man wakes up to discover he's turned into a cockroach, but that's exactly what I felt like. (I have a massive fear of cockroaches to this day, by the way—well, water bugs. Same thing. But I digress.) If I was afraid of my psoriasis at four, my

anxiety tripled at eleven. This was a life-changing event, not just internally but for everyone to see. I believed with sudden certainty that this time I wasn't just different—I was unfixable.

While I had carried around a nagging sensation from the time that I was four that I was "flawed," I don't know that I was prepared emotionally or psychologically to handle what happened at eleven. It stopped being about me not feeling quite right and became more about people treating me like I wasn't normal. I didn't look normal anymore. No more unnoticeable patches. It was like being outed for being a monster.

For all of sixth grade a red crust covered my entire body. My scalp was affected the worst, with layers of peanut brittle–thick scales beneath my hair. The only thing that seemed to help was a gooey, thick amber coal tar. My mom would rub it into my scalp, and I would sleep with a shower cap on so I didn't get it on the sheets. The following morning, she would put my head over the sink and scrub my hair and scalp with boric acid to remove the tar. This was an almost daily routine for a year. The process was time consuming because of my long hair, so we had to find a way to make it easier. One day I had hair down to the middle of my back, and the next, a crew cut. Getting my hair cut like that didn't just make me feel less girly—it made me feel less human.

Oddly, my face was unaffected by the psoriasis, which was a single saving grace. Otherwise, I would have had to wear a ski mask even in August.

I covered up as much as I possibly could, and I adopted a uniform during that period. Even on the hottest days, I wore turtlenecks and long pants—though I had to be careful with dark colors because of snowstorm-like dandruff that would fall onto my shoulders and eventually get over everything. I was hiding under my clothes, absolutely. Covering up did give me some feeling of control, but it wasn't a comfort or a joy. I missed my fancy dresses. If there are any pictures of me from that time, I have yet to find them. I didn't want to be seen, much less have lasting evidence of my appearance.

Kids that age are cruel, it goes without saying, and anyone who seems different is threatening. Different didn't begin to describe me. My classmates left notes in my locker telling me I was uglier than the Elephant Man. (Lucky me, the movie had just come out.) And truth be told, I felt just as deformed as he. Some of the kids' notes told me to leave school before I infected everyone. I think they were genuinely afraid they could catch what I had. The right-handed kids wrote with their left hands to disguise their handwriting, but I always knew who was sending them. (You know who you are . . . and so do I.)

In the middle of that year the panic attacks started. I would be twenty feet from the big red doors of the school and just not be able to move. My limbs would lock, and more often than not I'd start to cry. Some days, my parents forced me to go in; some days, they didn't. I wound up missing a lot of sixth grade. I used to be fantastic at math, but that year I fell behind and never bothered to catch up.

I started going for UVA/UVB light-therapy treatments at New York Hospital. The light booth reminded me of a *Star Trek* transporter. (Not to say I'm a Trekkie. I much prefer *Star Wars*. Darth Vader has awesome style.) Even though I wore protective eye goggles, the light would seep in through the bottom of the goggles. I was fascinated by the color: The ultraviolet light really *was* purple. Nice to know a favorite color from childhood was part of the cure.

For a few weeks that year I went to Boca Raton, Florida, to live with my grandmother and aunt. It was during this time that I learned that Boca style was not to be aspired to. (If you're from Boca, know that I still appreciate the hospitality you showed me, if not the orthopedic footwear.) My dermatologist thought that sun and salt water might help ease my symptoms, and they did, slightly. At Grandma's retirement community, Century Village in Deerfield

Beach, I met a fellow sufferer, an elderly gentleman in a wheelchair wearing shorts and a T-shirt. His psoriasis was even thicker than mine on his knees and elbows and patches of his shins. I'd never seen anyone with my condition and, I admit, it was a relief to know I wasn't alone. But the connection didn't last. The dude was old! I thought, *He's going to die soon.*

My dad came down for a visit. By then I was doing the natural version of light therapy by going outside to expose my scales to the sun for a few hours each day. (Just writing that makes me sound like an amphibian, aka Lizard Girl.) Ordinarily I'd confine myself to my aunt's pool, where no one could see me. But when Dad suggested we take a walk on the beach, I put on my bathing suit and joined him.

As we waded along in the surf I noticed an old woman in a floppy beach hat and sarong heading toward us. As she approached she smiled but then kind of . . . paused . . . at the sight of me.

She said to Dad, "I'm so sorry. What's *wrong* with her?"

I'll never forget the look on his face. He stammered a reply—I don't even remember what he said—and we turned around and left, his hand wrapped tightly around mine. He looked *so* upset. Thinking about it now, my heart aches for him. He was hurt for me. At the time, I felt guilty that I had ruined his day.

Many nights I'd sob to my parents

Dad is making tuna fish while I rock out to Stevie Wonder, also age ten

and ask, "Why do I have to be different? Why am I like this?" Now, as an adult, I have the utmost sympathy for how hard this must have been for them. Watching anyone suffer, but especially your child, and being powerless to help is an awful position to be in.

I barely looked at myself. I avoided mirrors and made deals in my head. I'd think, *If I could have normal skin, I'd give up my teeth.* Or, *For normal skin, I'd gain fifty pounds.* (Be careful what you wish for.) One of my most vivid memories of this period was of a department store dressing room. Mom had taken me to Bloomingdale's to shop, and I was trying on an awesome pair of lilac velveteen Gloria Vanderbilt jeans with an equally awesome red satin top. The color combo was brilliant, and remains one of my faves to this day. I was so distracted that I hadn't realized until I had the outfit on that the shirt had short sleeves. There was no way I could buy it, and I was crestfallen. (Even then, I preferred to buy complete outfits instead of separates.) As I took off the shirt, standing in the fluorescent lighting of the room, I looked at the splotches all over the right side of my rib cage. Seeing the disease all over me, in that situation, in that space, made me think: *There's no hope. I'll never get better.*

In fact, the research, at least then, did suggest that psoriasis gets worse as you age. While my fear at eleven that I would never be able to wear short sleeves may sound ridiculous—Who cares about a short sleeve?—right then, for me, it was like accepting that I'd never fall in love or be successful or accomplish anything. It felt like this . . . handicap . . . had taken over and it was going to determine my whole life. I felt hollow. That's the only way to describe what I now look back on as a combination of shock, disappointment, and resignation. There were so many things I'd never be able to do or have that everyone else was entitled

to simply by virtue of being alive. I saw my future: I would always be envious of people with normal skin.

At the beginning of seventh grade, and totally by accident, we found a "cure."

My family and I had gone to the movies to see either *Meatballs* or *Little Darlings*. (It was one of the two. They were my favorites, and they both took place at camp, although in *Meatballs*, none of the kids went all the way, only the counselors.) Just as we entered the theater, I had a sudden, intense outbreak on my bicep, near my elbow. The patch felt as if it were on fire. We always carried around a plastic bag filled with whatever gels and creams the doctors had most recently prescribed and by now had quite the inventory of tubes. I chose one randomly and applied it, and we went into the theater and watched the movie (which was awesome, whichever one it was. Both still are).

Back on the street afterward, my dad asked, "How's the patch?"

I realized I'd forgotten about it. I held up my arm to check, and stopped in my tracks: The flare-up hadn't just calmed down; it had almost disappeared. That one patch of skin looked almost normal.

We rushed home and emptied the bag of medicines on the kitchen table in a frenzy to try to find the ointment we had used. We somehow determined that it was a tiny sample tube labeled Diprosone. The next day Dad called the dermatologist to get a prescription for more of it.

"It's a topical steroid—a strong one," he said. "If it works, use it."

We got a prescription, and I slathered it all over my body, in generous amounts. Within three months almost every square inch of my psoriasis was gone.

Aside from that one instruction, we didn't get a lot more information about how to apply it. In retrospect it seems obvious that Diprosone came in those tiny little tubes because you weren't supposed to use a lot. I hadn't felt normal for nearly a year. The possibility that this skin condition wasn't a life sentence was overwhelming. I couldn't wait to get rid of it.

Even though the scales were gone, it took a while for my emotions to catch up. The fear of an outbreak was as stubborn as the psoriasis had been. Even after my skin cleared, it was still hard for me to remember that I could wear T-shirts and shorts without people flinching at the sight of me.

As my hair grew out, it came with a surprise addition: A silver streak appeared at my right temple, in contrast to my otherwise dark brown hair. I never knew if the pigment loss was due to the stress, the coal tar treatments, or the boric acid. But the streak stayed. Me, Cruella DeVil, and Rogue from *X-Men*. Wonder if they have psoriasis, too. (Mutant, and not exactly proud.)

Although my skin was mostly clear, I began to notice something new, and not good. At first, the marks were small cracks, like scrapes, or the birth of a stretch mark. But then they lengthened and deepened, and fissures appeared. My skin was tearing like a zipper all over my body but mainly underneath my arms, boobs, and upper thighs.

"What the hell is going on?" my dad boomed on the phone to the dermatologist.

Diprosone was so strong, and I'd used so much of it, that it had started to thin my skin. And now it was tearing apart like tissue paper, and it hurt like hell. There was absolutely nothing that could be done about it. I pulled back on the Diprosone, only dabbing it on hot spots that would still flare up on my elbows, at my hair line, behind my ears, on one particular lesion on my left shin. Unless I wanted skin grafts—which would have to wait until I stopped growing—I was going to have to live with the scars, big purpley ones that made my skin pucker. The ones under my arms got so deep that once I was asked if I'd had my arms *reattached*. I was a teenage girl with scars on my boobs: I lived in fear that boys would see them and freak. When I did start making out with them, it was always in the dark.

I had one recurrence of psoriasis at sixteen, as a result of getting strep throat. (So much for the wonder of penicillin!)

If Flock of Seagulls, The Cure, and the wardrobe from Flashdance had a baby. Tah-dah. Age fifteen, maybe?

It started at my wrist and crept up to my elbow on the inside of my arm. I had a panic attack that my friends would abandon me, but this time I immediately admitted to them what was going on. One friend said, "I don't care if your skin's green." It was a big moment for me: I was so relieved! There was a possibility I wouldn't always be shunned as an outcast.

I finally had my tonsils taken out at seventeen. After all those antibiotics and light treatments, my tonsils were still chronically infected with strep. Not only did the operation clear up my skin, but I haven't had an outbreak of psoriasis since.

The scars are still with me. And the emotional scars on the inside? Let me check . . . faded like the ones on my skin, but still there.

I wouldn't wish what happened to me on any child. It certainly wasn't the worst thing to befall someone, but it wasn't fun. And I do think I was radically changed by it. Sometimes I wonder about the girl I would've been if I'd had normal skin. Maybe she would have been good at algebra and trigonometry. Maybe she'd be a math teacher now (but a really well-dressed one, without dandruff).

Seriously? I do sometimes mourn for the girl I was, and the girl I might have been. But rationally I know that's a waste of time. I also know my unique adolescence made me who I am. I defined myself by my non-normalcy, by my *Something's wrong with me* mindset. How one defines oneself became a preoccupation with me, and I studied it in various forms (philosophy, psychology, and literature) in high school and college. And I think there's an argument to be made that what I do now—working with women to define and redefine themselves—is an extension of the same preoccupation.

Although I've accepted my scars, I don't always feel okay about them. Wearing bathing suits during vacations in the dead of winter is the worst. I'm white as a corpse, with a strange texture to my skin and deep tears in it. When I see other women in bikinis, I don't even notice whether or not they've got great bodies. What I see—all I see—is the skin I'll never have. That's what I envy. It's smooth and uniform in color, not blotchy and purple from overuse of steroids. No matter how much I've worked out in my life, which quite honestly has never been nearly enough, the tops and backs of my thighs are never toned, because the skin there is simply too damaged to become taut. While I have given up dwelling on the insecurity, it never goes away completely. I wish I could leave the house, head off to meet friends, go to work, engage in life, and not think twice about my body or what it went through. But I'm not sure that's possible for me. Instead, I think I've learned how to live alongside it.

From the beginning of seventh grade the reconnect to fashion was a slow-build back, with lots of extreme choices along the way. (My Robert-Smith-of-The-Cure days still make me cringe.) It wasn't until I reached college, though, that it really became clear to me that my preoccupation with style wasn't just a childhood distraction. My attraction to fashion was about being able to *choose* the skin I got to live in. My appreciation for what style can achieve took root and defined the course of my career.

When you acknowledge the less than perfect parts of yourself, something magical begins to happen. Along with the negative, you'll also begin to notice the positive, the wonderful aspect of yourself that you may not have given yourself credit for, or perhaps even been aware of."

ASHLEY

Dear Stacy:

My name is Ashley, and I'm 19 years old. I'm currently a pre-med student at the University of Texas majoring in biology. I have always wanted to pursue a career in the medical field since I was five because I wanted to help people. For the past couple of years, I have put my appearance on the back burner and have completely lost all confidence. I want to gain it back and feel beautiful again.

During my junior year of high school, I started struggling with eating disorders and depression. My boyfriend of several years cheated on me with one of my friends. It was an extremely devastating experience for me, and it made me analyze all of my flaws. Before this happened, I was always considered a "skinny girl," at 5'4" and 120 pounds. After I found out about the cheating, I decided I needed to lose weight and dropped down to 100 pounds in a matter of weeks. Shortly after that, I became severely depressed and began packing on the pounds at a ridiculous rate. Over the course of one year, I gained nearly 50 pounds.

The weight gain sent me into an even deeper depression. I used to put a great emphasis on my appearance, but after this whole experience, I just stopped caring. I used to have great fashion sense and always wore cute clothes. For the past two years, I haven't felt motivated to shop or plan outfits because of my weight gain. I really just want to feel beautiful again. I think that getting style advice would help with my confidence and to stop worrying about my weight holding me back from things I want to do.

Thank you!!!
Ashley

I chose Ashley purely from the heart. It's awful to feel as if you've lost control over your life and to try desperately to regain it. What I didn't know at twenty-one, and what Ashley doesn't know at nineteen, I can tell you at forty-two: Taking negative control, as in developing an eating disorder, keeps you from the things you want, while taking positive control, as in creating a personal style, can help you get them.

As soon as she walks into the studio, I'm struck by how beautiful Ashley is—and how she's completely unaware of it. Everything about her—how she moves, sits, speaks—feels tentative and quiet, and I immediately feel protective and empathetic toward her. Ashley oozes vulnerability. Eating disorders rob you of objectivity and positive feelings about your appearance. Whatever it is that they have taken away from Ashley, I hope this Start-over can help restore.

The other thing that strikes me about Ashley: Her skin is flawless, even without a drop of makeup. She's dressed in an orange T-shirt with a funny logo from a Texas restaurant, capri-length black leggings, and Chinese slippers that looked as if they'd been run over a few times by a bus and then eaten by a dog.

"I wear funny T-shirts to distract people," she says in response to my comment on her shirt.

Funny, I'm not distracted.

As we sit on the couch together, Ashley relaxes enough to tell me her story. "I was dating this guy, and he cheated on me with one of my friends. I felt really insecure after that. The weight loss was definitely a reaction to the betrayal," she says. "I lost a little weight, and felt more attractive, so I kept it up. I was working out a lot, too. I could squat two hundred pounds and bench ninety. The weight came off really fast. I wouldn't use the word 'anorexia.' I never really considered it that. I just wouldn't eat very much. At a sitting, I'd have a piece of fruit, or something small. I never ate alone, only in front of others. My parents noticed I was losing weight, and they were concerned. That stage only lasted a couple of months. I dropped about twenty pounds, to a hundred.

"After a few months of losing weight, I got depressed," she continues. "I started binge eating, and was totally out of control. I'd eat anything I could, especially Oreos. That was one of my go-to choices. Eating made me more depressed. After you eat a whole box of cookies in one sitting, you feel pretty low."

I have a long history of eating more than one whole box of cookies. I know what happens when you punish your body: It gets back at you. And that sense of control you had disappears.

"I didn't have any confidence or feel attractive at all. I just stopped caring about how I looked. Around this time, the boy resurfaced. I was stupid and went back. We didn't last long, though," she says.

It's not stupid to be in love, but love can make us do stupid things. The return of the Cheater probably worsened Ashley's self-esteem. When we allow others to control how we feel about ourselves, we give up an essential sense of power. Ashley couldn't control her boyfriend or, at the time, her eating. What she *can* control are the choices she makes now and how she presents herself to the world.

"My style was totally affected by all this," she admits. "I used to care a lot about how I looked. I'd describe my old style as adventurous, bold. I stayed up on

Weight whiplash: This is what happens when your weight swings so far (in either direction) and so fast that your mind can't catch up: You think you should look one way, but the mirror reflects something else. It's another disorienting and disturbing aspect of eating disorders: You look in the mirror and think, *Who is that?* The unfortunate reality is that weight travels faster than the speed of brain. It takes a while to adjust to any fluctuations in weight, for the eye to take it in, and the brain to process.

trends, and wore really cute stuff. After the cheating incident, though, I stopped getting joy out of it. When the depression and weight gain started, I completely gave up. What was the point? I never left the house. I didn't want to hang out or see anyone. It was a hard adjustment. I was so used to being outgoing and loved to do things."

And now?

"I don't recognize myself," she says. "My weight has gone down and up so fast, I can't keep up with it. I'm always so surprised when I look in the mirror that I avoid them."✳

No avoiding mirrors today, though. (Tough love.)

Nodding, Ashley says, "I'm here for a boost. I haven't had much confidence for two years. Now I'm a freshman in college, meeting new people in a new place. It's a chance for a fresh start. I haven't binged in months, and I'm not doing any fad diets. I want to get back on my feet, and feel confident again instead of covering myself up in oversize sweatpants and sweatshirts.

I want to feel pretty again and get my groove back."

Thank God she's a lot younger than Stella.

I Get It

The funny thing about my bout with anorexia (not ha-ha or weird, but ironic) was that people noticed me and said, "You're so skinny!" and "You look great!" They would hold open doors for me, thinking I didn't have the strength to hold them for myself, in effect complimenting me for being sick. When I gained weight, I noticed people stopped holding doors. No one complimented me on my weight gain. The more I shrank, the more visible I became. By making less of myself, I got more attention, which was a self-esteem-scrambling paradox. An eating disorder is a form of negative control, although it seems positive when it's happening. Once you go down that path, all forms of positive control, like those accomplished through style, don't feel possible.

Like so many women I've met, I've been at war with my body for a long time. In high school I ate whatever I wanted and was always about fifteen pounds overweight. It didn't really occur to me that if I stopped eating ice cream and cookies every day after school, I could lose weight. I didn't want to stop eating what I loved. I wanted to be skinny but not to work at becoming skinny. So I convinced myself that it would never happen.

I went to Vassar. Along with new bedding and my *Betty Blue* movie poster, I brought with me a body in pretty good shape. Like all college students, my social life centered around partying and eating, mostly the carb-laden cafeteria food and Tony Napoli's white pizza with sausage at 3:00 A.M. I gained the classic freshman fifteen. I held on to it for sophomore year, too. Just for safe keeping.

For my junior year abroad, I traveled to London. I loved it there and made lots of friends, and cute English boys asked me out. Being a poor student abroad, I ate sparingly, mostly because I spent my money on going out and buying High Street clothes. Ten pounds came off without my even trying. Unlike in college, which seemed familiar, London was the first time I got to reinvent myself.

I started my senior year at Vassar with two main goals: to write my senior thesis and to take concrete steps toward "improving" myself. I wanted to get a job in fashion after graduation, so I would have to start working toward looking the part. I wanted a boyfriend, so I would have to stop blaming being "fat" for not having one. My time abroad had given me self-assurance and shown me what was possible. I wanted that feeling to continue, and to finish college on a high note.

At the time, I weighed 134. My plan was to take three months to lose ten pounds. I'd work my tush off on my thesis and diet, and graduate feeling both brainy and thin. Looking back, it was strange that I wasn't more anxious about the huge academic pressure I'd set up for myself by attempting a very complicated thesis (humble brag, "Nietzsche, Thomas Mann, and Herman Broch, the Concept of Self and Its Relationships to the Creation of Character in Literature," and I threw in some Heidegger and Buddhist philosophy for good measure, too) or the prospect of entering the real world and having to find a job. Anxiety is slippery, though. You can think it's only about one thing and later realize it was about many things. All of my nervous energy was focused on creating the New Me.

The New Me, as it turned out, had only me for company. I couldn't go out and party because I had an 8:00 A.M. intensive German class every day; showing up hungover just wasn't an option. I soon stopped drinking altogether, and then stopped going out to dinner with friends. I quickly developed an uncanny ability to say a smooth "Thanks, no" when I was offered food or mints or chips or candy. Instead of meeting people for brunch, I'd suggest we get together for coffee.

About a month into the New Way, my fave black jeans with white topstitching from Reminiscence started to feel loose. My best friend noticed, and said, "You look really good. But are you okay?"

I was pleased by the compliment but surprised by the concern. "What do you mean?" I asked. "Of *course*. I'm *fine*."

I was living in a single room, so there was no one around to monitor my increasingly rigid eating. I started making sugar-free butterscotch pudding with fat-free milk, leaving in lumps of dry pudding mix for texture so there was something solid to chew. I would freeze it and eat that for breakfast every morning with two popcorn rice cakes. Lunch was gum, an Orangina, and one apple. Dinner was a single-serving can of tuna in water. If I did have to eat dinner out, it was a salad and salmon or just a bowl of soup. After my last bite of food for the day, my last thought would be: *Eat even less tomorrow.*

Everyone began to comment on how I

was becoming thinner, and they gave me compliments. Buoyed by all the positive feedback, I did something I hadn't done in ages: I stepped on a scale. *One hundred and fourteen* came up on the screen in LED numerals. I'd lost twenty pounds. I couldn't believe it! It hadn't even been that hard. This renewed my commitment.

As the weeks went by, though, and my weight continued to drop, I started to notice that some people seemed uncomfortable around me, which made me feel uncomfortable in turn. I reacted by spending more time alone in my room, or tucked away in the library with the excuse that I was working on my thesis. While I was buried in the stacks, my mind would inevitably drift to food. I spent hours thinking about all the things I craved, and began to keep a list of fantasy foods I'd eat again one day. I remember really missing PB&Js.

The phrase "eating disorder" came up for the first time over Thanksgiving. My best friend couldn't help but notice my weight loss and eating changes. She turned to me and said, "I think you have a problem. You might need help. Do you have an eating disorder?"

I laughed. "Don't be ridiculous!" There was no question in my mind that I was fine and that she was completely wrong.

But after the holiday my certainty took a hit. While I was hanging out with a bunch of people in the library area where you could smoke (those were the days!), I popped a stick of gum in my mouth and a friend asked, "Is that dinner?"

Everyone laughed. I was humiliated and unnerved, as if I'd been called out. Did they *all* think I had a serious problem—and, if so, that it was something to joke about?

Later that night I went to the psychology section of the library and found a book with a checklist of anorexia symptoms. The author suggested putting a check by each of the ones that applied.

- Refusing to eat and denying hunger. *Check.*
- An intense fear of gaining weight. *Check.*
- Negative or distorted self-image. *Check?* (How did you know if your body image was distorted if it actually *was* distorted?)
- Excessively exercising. *Uh, no.* (To this day, I hate exercising and rarely do it. The stationary bike in my dining room? Doubles as a clothing rack.)
- Preoccupation with food. *Double check.*
- Social withdrawal. *Check.*
- Thin appearance. *Check, I guess.*
- Dizziness or fainting. Now that I think of it . . . *check.*
- Frequently feeling cold. *Check.*

The list went on: Abdominal pain. Menstrual irregularity. I had them all. After checking nearly every box, I sat there stunned. *I'm anorexic?* I thought. *Impossible.* The list described symptoms but not *me.* I decided it wasn't a definitive diagnosis.

I went home for Christmas, stepped on the scale, and discovered I weighed 103 pounds. I was awestruck. If I'd been shaken by any fears that I might actually have an eating disorder, that number—so close to 100—gave me the will to stick with my plan. By the New Year, I was down to 98 pounds.

The thing about eating disorders is that once they take hold, they don't let go so easily. No matter how hungry I was, I could not allow myself to eat anything other than what I had prescribed. If I did, I'd lose control, and that would mean failure. And more than anything, I was terrified of that.

My sex drive, meanwhile, was nonexistent. If my diet began, in part, to get guys to like me, the effect rendered men irrelevant. Get laid? I was too tired for lip gloss. My style waned, too, and I let it slide. It took all my energy to power through classes and finish my thesis. When I accepted my Phi Beta Kappa key at the awards ceremony, I'd hit an all-time low of ninety pounds. I was twenty-two years old, five foot seven inches tall, and

At my graduation from Vassar

I weighed as much as a golden retriever. What began as a three-month plan to lose ten pounds had turned into nine months of obsession and isolation, and a precipitous plunge of almost fifty pounds.

At this skeletal weight, I interviewed at *Vogue* magazine in February of my senior year, and was offered the position of personal assistant to the executive fashion editor, to start after I graduated. At anywhere else other than Condé Nast, a size 00 anorexic would have been rushed to a hospital rather than escorted to the human resources department to fill out

About a year after graduation, with my dad

immune system was shot. I came down with double pneumonia one week before my start date at *Vogue*. My boss was very understanding, and promised to hold the job for me. According to the doctors, the only way I would get well was to eat.

So I started eating . . . and then I couldn't stop. Bedridden, I began shoveling down boxes of cereal and loaves of bread, and I gained weight fast. I was a wreck. As the pounds piled on, I was consumed with anxiety. What would the editors at *Vogue* think when they saw me? I was out of control. My body was conspiring against me again.

My start date had been postponed for two months. When my first day finally arrived in November 1991, I weighed 139 pounds. I'd gained forty pounds since my boss had last seen me. I was sure she wouldn't recognize me. Reintroducing myself to her, I was terrified. She didn't say anything about it, but I suspect she must have noticed.

As one of some ten or twelve assistants in the fashion department, I organized photo shoots, got props, coordinated the models, steamed clothes, and generally anticipated the needs of the editors. I tried to work hard to make up for my appearance. I was thirty pounds heavier than anyone else and felt deeply self-conscious and anxious about my weight. The worry only exacerbated my new compulsion—overeating.

a W-2 form. Of course, I was thrilled. I was going to work at *Vogue*? Legendary *Vogue*? And they were going to *pay* me? I'd landed a dream job on my first try. Anorexics are geniuses at finding justifications for their behavior, and getting this job was a great example of that. *If I weren't thin*, I told myself, *they wouldn't have hired me.*

And then my body simply gave out. After a year of starvation and stress, my

My new eating disorder, just like my old one, was secretive. During binges, I'd eat an entire Entenmann's raspberry loaf cake—all 1,800 calories of it—before bed. Saturated fat and sugar were my Ambien, leaving me with a blissful, heavy feeling that let me sleep. Or I'd devote an entire Saturday to eating it, piece by piece, mixing pleasure and shame the entire time.

The weight continued to pile on just as rapidly as it had come off the year before. I grew a dress size every month for a few months. By the time I left *Vogue* in 1993, I'd ballooned to 180 pounds. Within two calendar years my weight had, literally, doubled.

My two-year stint with eating disorders left me with a confused sense of self. My weight—and, to some degree, my identity—didn't stabilize for another seven years. Eventually, my metabolism kicked back in and I was able to reach a healthy, normal weight.

Eating disorders aren't exactly like alcoholism. I don't feel as if I'm one diet away from full-blown anorexia or one big meal away from cyclic bingeing. But I do have to be careful about my thinking. While in the throes, I couldn't understand that my real power wasn't derived from restricting and rewarding or that I wasn't psychologically beholden to the number on a scale. Now I know better—at least at the logical level. Emotions are hard to manage. Even now, twenty years later, I worry about my weight. I'm a fluctuator. I've gained fifteen pounds in the last year. And I worry about worrying. But I try not to let my weight dictate my whole life anymore. I try to stay in a healthy range.

It was hard as hell for me to come out of the dark place I'd been in. Ashley has only recently emerged from her own two-year trial with starvation and overeating. I wish there had been a guide for me, someone I could have looked to for any kind of advice—not necessarily psychological—to help show me a path: a sister-in-arms, a mentor, someone who could empathize. I never reached out to other people with eating disorders or researched support groups, and in some ways, I regret that. I hope I can be that kind of person for Ashley, and anyone else who reads this and has experienced something similar. What Ashley needs now is to rebuild her emotional fortitude and to start feeling like herself again.

Ashley's Start-over

THE SYMPTOMS:

Oversize and elasticized clothes, a permanent slouch

THE UNDERLYING CAUSE:

Emotional strength sapped by two years of struggling with eating disorders

THE PRESCRIPTION:

Infusion of badass style

Ashley needs a full-arsenal wardrobe, sartorial suits of armor that make her feel protected and strong. Her clothes should be body-conscious so that she can reconnect with her body today.

Badass Essentials include:

A LEATHER JACKET. Instant emotional bulletproofing.

HIGH HEELS. Ideally, big bad boots. Besides the fact that stepping into them makes you feel tough, when you wear heels, you can't slouch. Ashley tends to do that. Slipping into that posture comes from not feeling good physically, and trying to make herself appear smaller. Heels force us to stand up straight: shoulders back, boobs out, tummy in, ass out. Ashley

Thank God for platforms. They are by far the most comfortable high heel. The extra couple of inches at the ball of the foot cuts down on the amount of pressure you put on it. Your arch won't feel as steep. And you can get away with wearing five-inch heels that feel like three-inch ones.

> *If you layer with thinner fabrics, you can create visually interesting outfits without the bulk. Details like sheer fabrics are provocative and feel powerful without being outright obvious.*

When reacquainting yourself with a changed body, try everything before discounting anything: new fabrics, new colors, new accessories, new shapes.

needs the reminder that *it's okay to take up space. That's what we're here for.*

FITTED JEANS. Fitted *everything*. When Ashley wasn't treating herself well, she hid in baggy sweats. Now that she's starting to feel better, she should dress in fitted (but *not tight*) clothes to reinforce and remind her that her life and her mind-set have changed. Buying fitted, tailored clothes can often create some size anxiety, but you mustn't allow yourself to get stuck on a number. Wearing a size 8 that doesn't look good isn't half as powerful as wearing a size 12 that fits your shape. Go with whatever looks *good in the mirror*, regardless of size.

ACCESSORIES WITH TOUGH DETAILS. A studded leather belt. Some heavy metal jewelry. Sparkle. Anything that looks a little rocker.

ANIMAL PRINT. Don't choose just any animal print—leopard *roars*. Zebra, on the other hand, screams "Eat me." (Kidding. Any animal print has a little badass connotation.)

The process of creating an outfit allows you to see your present body more clearly. Give thought to the detail and take time with it. It's the same process as painting a picture. Assemble your pieces and your color palette. Ask yourself whether you have filled the canvas properly. Concentrating on building your outfit can help distract from any negative thoughts about your frame.

Have Fun!

Why This Works

Wow. That's (almost) all there is to say.

• **THE JACKET:** There is something about a well-fitted modern jacket that feels like armor. If it's cut well, it adds a dose of cool to anything you wear it with and does the heavy lifting when it comes to creating a flattering shape. Here, the lapel hits at Ashley's waist, which is emphasized by belting her jeans. The hem of the jacket sits lower on her hips, slimming them.

• **THE BLOUSE:** *Meow.* Animal print adds some edge to Ashley that contrasts with her "good girl" looks. Because the print consists of neutral colors, it works well when paired with brights. (I love printed button-down shirts, when a larger chest is not an issue, under crewneck solid-color sweaters as well. All you see is the collar and cuff—a more subtle way to wear the print but still add some pop.)

• **THE JEANS:** Ashley needed to see herself in a modern-cut jean, with a straight leg and slightly higher rise, in the right size. She couldn't believe she could wear a shirt tucked in! She'd been hiding her shape in oversize tees and elastic-waist leggings for too long. The moment she put on a jean that fit properly, her waist looked trim and her legs were a kajillion miles long. (A word about "pooling": When a jean is long, it is perfectly acceptable to let the jean "pool" or wrinkle on the top of the boot or shoe as long as it doesn't weigh the look down. If it starts looking too bunchy, just hem the jean a couple of inches for a less bulky look.)

• **THE BOOTS:** Nothing says "Yep, I am a baller" better than a great ankle boot. They work with jeans, trousers, even skirts and dresses. Here they give Ashley's look a tougher edge with a platform and add an exclamation point to the end of the outfit "sentence."

THE COLORED-JEAN CONTROVERSY

For the last few years, colored jeans have become more and more popular. And more and more, women ask me if they can wear them. In general, the super trendy stuff is targeted at women in their late teens, twenties, and early thirties. But a trend like this is one in which anyone at any age can participate. Jeans are jeans—as long as the cut is flattering on you, the color won't scream "too young." Just remember: most colored (and printed denim) is cut in a skinny leg style. If you carry extra weight in your lower half, this *cut* (regardless of the color or print) will be less flattering than a straight leg or trouser leg jean.

Yes!..............And?

Accept the unvarnished truth and build your style strategy from there.

"I don't recognize myself."

Give it time. As hard as it is to look at yourself after a big weight gain or loss (or both), you only make it harder by not doing so. A great way to realign the mind is to look at yourself—naked and in clothes—in a full-length mirror. You have to stay with your reflection until you do recognize yourself, know yourself, and accept yourself. If you avoid it, there will always be a disconnect between what you can see, and what you actually are.

"My confidence is gone."

Losing confidence at nineteen is awful—and typical. You don't have to be cheated on or have an eating disorder to feel bad at that age. A favorite quote of mine from Marcus Aurelius: ". . . be like the rock that the waves keep crashing over. It stands unmoved and the raging of the sea falls still around it." To me, it means, stay centered and still in the storm, even if you can only do it 80 percent of the time. Wearing clothes that give you confidence can prop you up, and do some of that work for you. It's one way to be kind to yourself as you find your center again and rebuild your self-worth.

"I want to feel beautiful again."

You are already beautiful. At any weight. When you have style, you leave open the door for opportunity. When you dress for the job you want instead of the job you have, you're actualizing your desire. If you can see it, you can believe it, and vice versa. It's about believing in your own happiness, or beauty—not just recognizing it, but *feeling* it. Style is the means that lets that feeling back in.

And one more thing (to quote Steve Jobs): Though it seems like I'm contradicting myself here, the last ingredient to feeling beautiful is to STEP AWAY from the mirror. You need to see yourself reflected in other people's eyes—people who love you, are rooting for you, are proud of you. Discover what it is you love again outside of style, having nothing to do with what you look like. What are your goals? What do you want to achieve? Sometimes the best way to reconnect with an essential sense of self-esteem is to put down the lip gloss, step away from the jeans, and turn your back on the mirror. The things you do to establish your identity and help you develop your sense of self, in turn, develop your sense of style. Your self-esteem can't come from how you look alone. Feel kind, successful, and accomplished. The whole package IS beauty. And then your decisions about how to wrap the package are a direct transla-tion of who you are. Confident people dress confidently.

SIZE DOESN'T MATTER

Don't be psychologically attached to a number, be it size, weight, or age. What you see is what you are. No one is going to reach in and check the size label in your pants. Even if they did, you could always cut out the labels. Or take a Sharpie and cross out the 1 on a 12, and—presto—you're a 2!

And remember, you'll be a different size in almost every label you try on. Every designer cuts sizes differently, which makes the numbers meaningless. Check out this clothing size chart, care of Net-a-Porter.com:

	XXS	XS	S	M	L	XL	XXL	XXXL
ITALY	38	40	42	44	46	48	50	52
UK	6	8	10	12	14	16	18	20
US	2	4	6	8	10	12	14	16
FRANCE	34	36	38	40	42	44	46	48
JAPAN	5	7	9	11	13	15	17	19
DENMARK	32	34	36	38	40	42	44	46
AUSTRALIA	6	8	10	12	14	16	18	20

You might be a 10 in America, but in England (or in clothes by English designers), you're a 14. The number doesn't matter. What matters is how you look in the clothes.

"There is only one you in the world, just one,
and if that is not fulfilled then something wonderful
has been lost."

—MARTHA GRAHAM

TY

Stacy,

Here's my story: In high school, there was not one trendy store for me to shop in. Because I was tall and curvy at the age of 12, I shopped with my mother at Fashion Bug and Kmart in the Missy section, which I affectionately renamed "Granny's Closet." I became the jokester of my crew to distract them from my lack of stylish clothes. For prom, I wore a plus-size bridesmaid gown. The cute poufy girlie dresses didn't have enough material for my size DD bust and 52 inches of hip.

Fast forward to age 35. I still have the same problems. Fashion doesn't fit. Have a peek inside of any magazine or at the cover. No one looks like me! I'm your average cute, curvy brown girl, not the light-skinned, tall, weaved model type. As a fashion and beauty blogger, I attend New York Fashion Week each season with the demoralizing task of reporting on clothes I drool over, but can't afford or fit into. There's not one good reason why I don't see my reflection in fashion. By writing about the issue, maybe I can help change it.

I claim to be an authority in fashion, and I have a good eye——for other people. I have no clue where to find stylish clothes for myself. Nothing ever fits, and I have no money for new fall items. All my funds are being exhausted living out my Carrie Bradshaw dreams in the city that never sleeps.

xoxo,

Ty

At first look, Ty is not at all what I was expecting. In the photo she sent with her letter, she was standing in a cutesy pose. But when she arrives at the studio, she is dressed like a teenage boy, wearing a zip-up hoodie, skinny jeans and Chuck Taylor navy sneakers. I keep looking behind her for the skateboard. In striking contrast to the Bieber outfit is the fact that her hair is all salt and pepper. Not that I don't dig it—I just couldn't see that in her photo. From her letter, I was expecting someone trying to embody her concept of great style. But instead, she looks like she's opted out of style, period.

I sense that her guard might be up, too. Or maybe she's just tired—it's early in the morning, after all. As the day progresses, though, Ty loosens up. Her smile is infectious. She's quick to laugh, and so funny. In retrospect, she might have been reserved at first because she hadn't had her coffee.

"I was plus-size very young," she begins our conversation. "We didn't have a lot of money, so I shared clothes with my mom." *Bells! Whistles! Alarms!* ✳ "I made a lot of jokes about what I wore back then, like the mom jeans, as a defense mechanism. It was hard. Mom was big. I was big. There weren't a lot of stores

✳ **When a grown woman tries** to capture a feeling she didn't have as a child with her clothes, she's setting herself up to fail. I see this phenomenon a lot. Women who wore nothing but hand-me-downs as kids might become shopaholics as adults, for example. Or women who were forced to be super- modest as kids grow up to dress like sluts. It's the rebellion syndrome. I can't stress strongly enough how a teen shopping in the same stores as her mom can warp her sense of style. Ty associates plus-size clothing with that dowdy feeling from her teens and into her twenties. Now that she's making her own decisions, it seems clear that she's rebelling hard against frumpwear. But trying to capture a feeling she was denied in the past doesn't make the best use of what she has now, in the present.

available to us, so I was limited to Lane Bryant and Ashley Stewart, and all my friends wore cute girlie clothes."

A teenager wearing mom jeans—literally, her own mom's jeans? There's an awesome therapy book in there somewhere.

"Around ten years ago, when I was twenty-five, I got a boyfriend who wanted me to dress better," she says. "Not in a mean way. We'd get ready to go out, and he'd put on jeans and a blazer. I'd put on a frumpy dress and he'd say, 'Are you wearing *that*? You're so pretty, you should put on something nice.'"

Thank God for Mr. Right. Nothing wrong with dressing to make your honey proud.

"But I struggled with it. I went to stores. I shopped online. But nothing fit. Plus-size brands only carry the stuff I hated wearing as a kid," she says. "I dressed old as a teenager. My hair went prematurely gray in my twenties. I'm in my thirties now, and I want to feel and dress young. I don't want to look like I'm fifty! I want to wear that stuff the trendy girls wear. For a while now, I've been shopping at juniors stores that carry plus sizes. I should be able to show people that a plus-size woman can be stylish, too."

Of course, they can. But Ty's strategy is not the best way to prove it. A store targeting teenagers is not going to be appropriate for a thirty-five-year-old.

*Of course, money makes it seem easier to have style. But while high-designer items may cost a lot of money, style has no price point. I remember being in my twenties, counting out change for cat food, but loving my $30 pants from H&M. I was so broke at one point, I had to borrow $16 from my boyfriend to buy the pan to cook him dinner at my place. In Ty's case, it's time to stop blowing through her clothing budget snapping up cheap, trendy crap at juniors stores, and invest in one or two higher-quality items that are cut for her body and stage of life. FYI, I'm not knocking juniors stores. They do have a lot of cute clothes—for *juniors*. For a thirty-five-year-old woman with dreams about working in the fashion business? Shut. Up.

Juniors clothes aren't cut for the body of a grown woman even if they are available in her size. Plus isn't simply about size: It's about shape, too. It requires a different pattern altogether. Junior brands that expand their size range aren't cutting for a plus-size *shape*. Ty's present style transmits a kind of desperation to be young and trendy. It's a visual disconnect from the reality of her body and age.

"I love fashion," she says. "I follow all the trends for my fashion/beauty blog. I have a great eye, but I can't seem to apply it to myself. I have excellent style, but for other people. It seems like, in the fashion world, which I'm trying to get a foothold in, you either have a gajillion dollars and no taste, or lots of taste and no money. I've got taste, but not enough money," she says. *

*✱ **You can't dress** in every trend, even if you want to be in the fashion industry. Dressing well doesn't mean following the pack. It means knowing what does and doesn't work on you.*

Not having money isn't necessarily a life sentence. What are her professional goals?

"My ultimate dream is to write for fashion magazines," she says.

"Somewhere like *Vogue*?" I ask.

"No," she says firmly. "*Vogue* doesn't speak to me."

So why, I wonder, isn't she speaking to *them*? Why write off *Vogue*, an industry leader, when her own mission statement is to see more people in fashion who look like her? She could be a trailblazer. Ty's current look puts her at a distinct disadvantage, though. The reality is, it's unlikely any fashion magazine would hire her based on how she dresses now. Her dismissal of *Vogue* feels like a preemptive rejection rather than a clearly thought-out assessment of her potential career choices.

"I try to dress for the world I want to be in, but I'm not sure of myself there," she says. "I went to a lunch yesterday for a product launch. I spent hours trying to decide what to wear. I changed my mind three times and decided on a rocker-ish pink sweater and jeans. I got there, and everyone was wearing gorgeous little

dresses. I almost had an anxiety attack. It's a terrible feeling, to walk into a room and want to turn around and walk out. I'm trying to wear what will make me feel like I fit in, but even though I'm doing what I think I should be doing, the confidence isn't there."

If Ty wants to fit into a particular world, the best thing she can do for herself is to stop trying to match her peers, or anyone else, and find an appropriate outfit for her and the world she wants to conquer. Why would any of us want to look or dress just like everyone else? ✱ Anyone who has followed me on Twitter or heard me speak knows I refer to each of us as "snowflakes." It's our differences that make us unique. (If it weren't so damn cheesy, I'd have called this book *Snowflake Style*.) Ty seems to be trying to come up with a generic fashion-blogger costume to feel secure in her role. But if she had a unique strategy (not unlike the unique structure of a snowflake), her colleagues might respect and admire her for it. There is only one Ty.

I, for one, totally respect Ty's goal to represent all the women who feel that *Vogue*—and the fashion industry in general—doesn't speak to them. Any worthy challenge to the status quo is going to take effort and determination. As a plus-size woman in a community of X rays, Ty certainly has her work cut out for her. She needs to see herself as a trailblazer with a distinctive voice in fashion—and to dress with the individual flare to shift her perspective. She has to throw away the style playbook she's been using and write a new one.

"But how?" she asks.

But how: Two words that eloquently express the frustration of trying. So many women want to reach their full style potential, to feel as confident as they rightfully should, and then simply don't know how to do it. As always, the "how" starts with *you*: What do you love about yourself, and what makes you happy to wear?

A major factor in Ty's favor? She loves her body.

"I like my hips," she says. "And I love my 'girls.'"

What makes her happy to wear?

"Sequins," she says. "They make me feel fancy."

Oh, goodie. Sequins are one of my specialties.

I Get It

There was a time in my life when not feeling as if I were in the right place was actually warranted. One of those occasions was in a small space—an elevator. The only other passenger was Anna Wintour. And if you don't know who she is, Google her.

I hadn't been working at *Vogue* for long. From the start I felt awkward there. I was the biggest girl in the fashion department—well, on the entire floor, perhaps in the entire building. My colleagues would complain about feeling fat if they couldn't slip into a 4, and I was tugging myself into a 14. I compared myself constantly to the other assistants, the models, the editors. They were all slim and gorgeous. And I was . . . working as hard as I could. With my head down, I rushed into an elevator one day, and found myself alone with the big boss.

Had I known the unofficial rule that you just didn't get into an elevator with Anna unless you were really psyched about your outfit and had a healthy ego, I'd have stayed at my desk for a few more minutes until I knew the coast was clear. But that day I stepped into the elevator after her. The door shut, and we rode down from the thirteenth floor. The entire ride took maybe ten seconds. It felt like ten years. When I managed to lift my eyes up from the floor, I could just make out hers behind her sunglasses, looking me up and down, up and down. I broke out in a sweat. Thankfully, I was wearing my Agnès B. houndstooth-print shirt with shiny silver buttons, and she couldn't see that my armpits had soaked completely through. Not one word was uttered, but the silence was deafening. To this day, I have no idea how she felt about the rest of my outfit, especially my teal Express stretch stirrup pants, but I'm going to go with "not good."

Since I left *Vogue*, I've spoken with her a few times, and she couldn't have been lovelier. But I don't think it was paranoia on my part to think that when she checked me out in that elevator, she was wondering, *Who the hell hired this girl?* I hope no one in human resources got fired.

I had a similar "one of these things is not like the others" experience at a Calvin Klein fashion show for the season's new collection of his diffusion line. I was backstage, assisting a stylist. My job was to "call the show," or make sure all the models were in the right outfits, in the right order, before they went out on the runway.

Standing to my left was Carolyn Bessette, a publicist for Calvin Klein at the time. Standing to my right was Kate Moss, the face of Calvin Klein, and first in the line of models.

While we waited for the show to start,

Carolyn said, "I went skiing with John this past weekend. He's so much better than me." (FYI: Carolyn's "John" was Mr. Kennedy Jr.)

Kate replied (English accent), "I went skiing with Johnny last month, and I was so much better than him." (FYI: Kate's "John" was Mr. Depp.)

So there I was, standing between two of the most beautiful women in the world, talking about arguably, two of the most beautiful men in the world, and I was thinking, *What the fuck am I doing here?*

I don't think I'm overstating it to say I didn't fit in in that world—not then, not now. I had to find my own path.

Back then, I believed that a job in the exclusive fashion industry would make me cool. People I met were impressed when they learned I worked at *Vogue*. But dealing day-to-day with the Carolyns and Kates? It was rough. Insecurity about my place was a constant. I was crippled by Sunday night "fraidies," what Audrey Hepburn as Holly Golightly in *Breakfast at Tiffany's* called "the mean reds." I would lie awake at night, wondering how I would walk into the office (again), face the beautiful skinny women (again), and find new ways to make fun of myself (again)? When I left fashion editorial and started working in commercials and advertising with real women, actors and models, women with imperfect bodies and limited resources, I began to feel a different kind of connection to my work. The alienation I had experienced at *Vogue* should have been a sign that I was meant to do something else—or the same thing but approach it differently. I had to find my own way. When I did, I was happier, and more successful, too.

Ty's Start-over

Clothing inappropriate to age and profession

Misguided desire to be trendy not frumpy, frustrated by lack of available options

Learning to see plus as a plus

Ty is a perfect example of someone who knows something's wrong and needs a little nudge to close the authenticity gap, to stop trying to follow the path of others, and to blaze her own trail. When you wear something that flies in conflict with your reality (for example, a thirty-five-year-old plus-size fashion blogger dressing like a scrawny sixteen-year-old barista at Starbucks), you don't look current or fashionable. You look kinda weird or, worse, desperate. (Sorry, the truth about style sometimes hurts.) Personal style is rooted in the individual. I can see Ty as a trailblazer in the fashion blogosphere if she can define her unique style and then wear the hell out of it. True confidence and feeling like you own any room you walk into comes from wearing clothes that reflect who you are. Ty is a big-hearted, beautiful, brave woman who loves sequins and her curves. If she gets back to her BASICs, she'll do herself justice.

BODY. Identify your body shape. Ty can take her plus-size pride and express it in style.

AGE. The goal should always be to look good for your age, not to look as if you are chasing your youth. Nothing screams "out of touch with reality" more than trying to look twenty years younger than you are. If Ty wears a sophisticated dress that's cut for her body, she can jazz it up with juniors accessories. (Who doesn't love a good Forever 21 or Topshop earring for less than $20?)

SELECTION. Use your eye not only to spot trends of the season, but to define the terms of your style. Know what to try on, as well as what to pass on.

INCOME. Your mantra should be quality over quantity: No more cheap stuff that

You might not be able to tell—a picture doesn't do it justice—but that shirt is shiny. Even though Ty loves sparkle and sequins, she has to be strategic about placement. The eye gravitates to shine, as it reflects light. If you want to highlight something, put shine there. If you want to camouflage it, go with matte.

falls apart in the wash. If you buy one quality item that'll last, it's more valuable than six crappy pieces that won't. In Ty's case, a pair of quality jeans that flatter her body might cost three times as much, but they'll last longer, look richer, and feel a hundred times better. Wherever she shops, she should choose whatever looks expensive. Also, always figure in the cost of tailoring into the price of a garment. A good rule for everyone: If you like a $39 pair of jeans, then you'll love them after you spend another $10 to have them hemmed properly.

How to do texture: On a budget, real fur is out of the question. Personally, I prefer synthetic fur anyway. (I don't want to wear a little furbie on my back.) You can buy synthetic fur that looks and feels a lot like the real thing. Use it as a go-to piece to wear with trousers, or to make a pair of jeans look more sophisticated. Warning: Fur can add bulk. On this piece, the pile is short. Ty gets the bang of fur, the visual impact of it, without the bulk.

CAREER. As an up-and-coming freelancer in fashion, Ty doesn't have to follow anyone's rules (except mine). She writes a fashion blog; she doesn't work at a bank. Conservative clothes aren't a necessity for her. A hot dress? Awesomesauce. At lunches or events, she can play up her independence and her uniqueness. Fashion should be fun, and she loves sparkle. So she should get dresses with strategically placed shine. She has to stop worrying about what everyone else is wearing, and just dress authentically.

Ty needs a higher-rise jean, one that locks and loads her midsection without being the equivalent of a girdle. (Repeat: Jeans are not girdles.) Plus-size jeans take into account a wider midsection. The ones carried by juniors stores, even up to size 20, are just larger version of a smaller-size cut that don't account for a midsection. That doesn't work for Ty's body shape.

Accessories must be proportional with your frame. For plus-size women, that means a thicker belt, bigger bag, scarf, and jewelry. Tiny accessories get lost on a frame like Ty's. The same rule for accessories holds true for prints. The print needs to match the stature of the woman who's wearing it.

I used to believe that one should only buy high-designer shoes for the quality and construction. Many times you get what you pay for. But these days there are so many reasonably priced well-made brands, you don't need to bust the piggy bank. Shoes are a game changer for any basic outfit. So even if you play it safe when it comes to your clothing, be bold and adventurous in your footwear!

Why This Works

• **THE DRESS:** A dress is a quintessential piece Ty needs to invest in. I chose this one for its attitude and versatility. It's got a universally flattering V-neckline, and shows some date-night cleavage. Layered with a lace camisole underneath and a blazer, it's great for day. Wear with boots and opaque tights to a lunch. Pseudo-neutral colors, like burgundy, can be paired with neutrals, or brighter colors, or print accessories. And the shoulder patches are black sequins. (Touchdown.) They visually broaden her shoulder and make her waistline appear smaller.

• **THE SHOES:** A chunky platform or thicker heel is more proportionate for a heavier calf than a pinpoint stiletto. Ty loves shiny, so the patent leather makes her very happy. They are also handy for killing water bugs. Fact.

• **THE BELT:** A wide belt underneath the bust, at the bottom of the rib cage, creates a smaller waistline for Ty. Placed above her natural waistline, it also makes her legs appear longer.

• **THE JEWELRY:** Ty can change these pieces up to be more casual or formal. Note the size of the pieces—bold and proportional to her frame. They don't get lost.

• **THE BAG:** Evening clutches are an exception to the proportion rule. Small ones work for evening regardless of body proportion. But feel free to use a larger one if you feel the need to carry tons of crap!

• **THE HAIR:** It bears noting that while I didn't expect Ty to have salt-n-pepper hair—I love it. It was the shape that didn't quite make sense. Her new cut was more about refining the look she was attempting to capture and bringing it into focus by truly giving her a Mohawk style. Committing wholeheartedly to a more angular cut really focuses the feel Ty's going for: girly and gutsy at the same time.

A WORD ABOUT SHAPEWEAR

Regardless of size, women should have a varied wardrobe of shapewear in their arsenal to smooth and tone natural lumps and bumps that don't always look flattering in form-fitting clothes. There is ZERO shame in wearing whatever smoothes things out and makes you feel your best. I always say, "Use what you got, then go get what you need." We all need some help from time to time! Banish the PMS bloats, the vacation indulgences, etc. Slimmers come in a range of "strengths" from a light hold to industrial armor.

Yes! . . . . And?

Accept the unvarnished truth and build your style strategy from there.

"I'm 35."

The thirties is the best decade ever. You're no longer struggling with the insecurity of your twenties, or the responsibilities of your forties. You're in the prime of your emotional, professional, intellectual growth. You're still young enough to go out drinking all night *and* go to work the next day looking good. Stylewise, you can wear a mix of youthful accessories with classic grown-up pieces. It's the best of both worlds.

"I'm plus size."

This is a challenge. Like any marginalized sizing, there's a complicated web of reasons that most designers don't make plus-size lines. To produce them, the patterns need to be cut differently, which requires creating an almost entire new line of clothes—an expensive proposition. This all sends a bad message: If you want to wear the clothes, change your body. That won't do. All I can say is the landscape is changing. Not only are small designers producing plus-size collections, so are major brands targeted at women in their twenties and thirties and truly cut for a plus-size shape.

"No one looks like me."

Compare and despair. I can't lie. This is a Twelve-Step mantra. The grass is going to be greener, in some way, on every person you see. They have the body you want, or they're younger, prettier, richer, etc. Instead of driving yourself nuts about it, stop it. Wanting anything other than what is yours is not only unrealistic, it only ends in despair. You can't be anyone but you. Set goals for *self*-improvement. Make your body as good as it can be. Be the best person you can be. But leave the rest of humanity to their own issues or you'll make yourself miserable trying to define yourself by what you're not vs. what you are.

ADMIRE OR ACQUIRE?

As a lover of fashion, Ty drools over clothes on the runway, in magazines, and in the movies. We all do. The fashion industry makes us mad with lust, and inspires us to open our wallets. But style isn't about copying a celebrity's choices; it's about learning from them. Using Ty as an example:

Q: Gwyneth Paltrow is jaw-dropping in an haute couture Tom Ford white dress on the red carpet. What inspiration can Ty take from her?

A: Not much. No matter how much you might admire a star's outfit, you shouldn't attempt to acquire it if you have a completely different body shape. That's a waste of your time and money. We can all admire Gwyneth's stunning style. But acquire it? Not possible, for 99 percent of us. Instead, take cues from Octavia Spencer, who wore a silver diagonally sequined gown with cap sleeves to the Oscars, and killed it.

Q: Zoe Saldana wears an orange backless gown to the Golden Globes. Again, one would think there isn't much to copy from such an outfit.

A: Not so! Zoe Saldana has a similar skin tone. Although Ty might not want to go quite so bare with nowhere to hide a supportive bra, frankly, she can look at Zoe's color choices and possibly acquire clothes in that hue that are cut for her shape.

Q: Christina Hendricks wears a bright pink floral print dress on *Mad Men* that emphasizes her eye-popping hourglass figure. Ty has curves, but not Christina's tiny waist. Forget the retro look?

A: Not at all. Ty can pick and choose elements of Christina's style that do match her body type. They're both well endowed on top. They both have hips. Ty can look for dresses with a similar shape, but with fabrics that have some stretch or give to them. Further, she can add a slimmer and wear a belt to deemphasize her midsection but keep all the hourglass curves she and Christina share.

"We have two options . . . give up or fight like hell."

—LANCE ARMSTRONG

JANIS

Dear Stacy:

My story starts back in August 2010 when I went for a yearly checkup and mammogram. That is when my life changed forever. I was diagnosed with Stage 2 breast cancer. Because of the type of cancer—lobular, which has a tendency to show up in both breasts—I was advised to get a double mastectomy with reconstruction of implants. I got second and third opinions. They all agreed. My mastectomy was on September 20, 2010.

From that day on, until reconstruction was complete on June 24, 2011, my life was a whirlwind of doctors, surgeries and medications. I never said, "Why me?" I feel blessed that I didn't need hardcore chemo or radiation, and my doctors were wonderful.

My problem now is being on Tamoxifen, a hormonal pill. One major side effect is weight gain. Despite going to the gym and walking regularly, I've put on sixteen pounds, going from 129 to 145. The extra weight and new breasts are making it very difficult to dress my new body. Trying to wear clothes from pre-cancer days just isn't working out. Tops just don't lay right. I'm thrown by the inconsistency in sizing. I did go for a bra fitting after reconstruction, but I'm not sure even that is right. UGH. Besides all that, I turned 60 last week. LOL. I'm frustrated, confused and really don't know where to turn for some guidance.

Thank you and best wishes,
Janis

The

first thing that strikes me about Janis is the surprising strength of her hugs. A great big bear hug from a small woman. She's like a firecracker, full of energy. I expected everyone to have a smile to meet me, that's just polite, but hers is huge and genuine. Not that I had previous expectations, but there's a tough Jersey girl attitude about her that I just love. You can see why this woman kicked cancer in the teeth.

"I really went through a lot after my surgery and reconstruction," she says. "It hasn't been easy. If I can help one other woman who's struggling find some short cuts and not go through what I did, I'd be thrilled."

I'm surprised that her number-one desire is to help others. I picked her because of her health crisis. Breast cancer in particular is a difficult recovery, and style is one way to reconnect to your body after fighting with it. But Janis's altruism is a benefit for the book, and the people who read it.

"I just turned sixty. I've been married for twenty-eight years. No kids, no grandkids," she says. "My husband and I both work full time—I sell airplane parts—but we go on a lot of vacations. It's a great life." *

A great life that was rudely interrupted by cancer.

"I was diagnosed at a routine checkup. I hadn't felt a lump. It was just good luck that my doctor noticed it. I had an ultrasound and a biopsy. It came back positive. Less than a month later, I had a double mastectomy," she says. "Before the operation, I said to the surgeons, 'I'm going in with breasts, and I want to come out with breasts.' So after removing

---

* Sixty years old? Shut the front door. I wouldn't have guessed her age. Looking youthful can be the result of being a genuinely happy person. Like Audrey Hepburn once said, "Happiest girls are the prettiest."

them, he put in tissue expanders under the chest-wall muscle, and pumped them up. The permanent implants came a few months later.

"I'm not quite done with the reconstruction. I just had nipples put on. The very last thing is to have areolas tattooed around them," she explains. It sounds like an ordeal. "It *was* an ordeal. But I think of myself as blessed. It was a close call. The type of cancer I had doesn't normally show in screenings. Because it was caught early, I didn't have to have chemo or radiation. I got to keep my hair."

Most people probably wouldn't call themselves "blessed" after a double mastectomy and painful reconstruction. Janis's positivity is impressive.

"I never said, 'Why me?' I told my husband, 'I don't want a pity party.' I'm just not a doom-and-gloom person. I take care of the problem and move on," she says. "I didn't take one pain pill. I was uncomfortable and sore, but nothing I couldn't handle.

"For the first six months after the diagnosis, I woke up every day terrified of a recurrence. That fear has faded somewhat, but it'll always be in the back of my mind," she admits. "I did my first Survivor Walk this year, although I don't think of myself like that. I had surgery and reconstruction, that's it. My husband yells at me, 'You *are* a survivor!' But my cancer

wasn't as dramatic as some other people's. I've been to support groups and met women who have had horrific experiences. It feels wrong to put my experience and theirs in the same category. I didn't ever feel sick."

But Janis was sick. And she experienced a kind of loss.

"My body has totally changed because of it," she says. "I have no idea how to dress now. Whenever I go shopping, I say, 'Where's Stacy London when I need her?' My breasts are hard. They're positioned higher than they were before. They're bigger. I have more cleavage. They look strange, like mounds. If you bend forward with normal boobs, they change shape, come to a point. But my new boobs don't move at all. Nothing fits right. I had a bra fitting after surgery, but I'm convinced it's wrong. I wound up a cup size bigger. And whatever size they are, the reconstructed breasts don't conform to a bra. Sweaters and shirts don't fall right. I get folds by the arms. I have scars, too. I know they'll fade, so that's not so bad. The worst part is that my new nipples—which are little bundles of skin—never go down. The nipples are tiny. But they're always hard."

Janis says, "Touch 'em."

Okay. It's always nice to cop a feel when you have permission. Still, the fact that she's offering them up for me to touch suggests she doesn't really feel they're a

*The best breast invention known to womankind: nipple petals. They're small silicone patches—I like the heart-shaped ones, but they come in flower and circle shapes too—that stick right on your nips. I wear them constantly. Instant low beams. No one will suddenly ask, "Is it really cold in here, or is it just you?"

part of her. It reminds me of when women who've had augmentation pull up their shirts to show it off. Women who haven't had any breast work done are less apt to show and tell; for them it feels more like flashing. *

"I don't feel much at all, because the nerve endings were cut," Janis says. "When I touch them, I feel pressure but no sensation. I know they're there and that they're mine. But they're not *me*. They feel as if they've been attached to me. My husband says, 'I'm not a boob man.' He's wonderful, and I'm sure he's fine with my new breasts. He says they look good. As far as being intimate is concerned, it's not the same for me."

I can't imagine how difficult this must be. The change in intimacy has nothing to do with the love Janis and her husband feel for each other and everything to do with the loss of her breasts. This isn't to say style can fix this, completely. It doesn't make nipple sensation come back.

But finding the right style can be the first step to reintegrating her new breasts with her whole body. If she can *see* that integration, she can begin to feel it.

"I'm glad people tell me I look good," she continues. "But I have to live with seeing myself in a different way. Obviously, it'd be worse for someone who lost a leg or an arm. Their loss is visible to the world. Mine isn't. I put clothes on, and no one knows. But I know what I've lost. There's that 'not the same' feeling. I had my breasts for fifty-nine years. They're gone, and I'm mourning for them. Time does heal. But my breasts are never coming back."

Janis also has to deal with other physical changes.

"Yes, I lost my breasts, and gained seventeen pounds. Weight gain is a common side effect of taking Tamoxifen. It makes my bones hurt, too. I've been taking it for one year, with four more to go. I'll be sixty-four when I finish. Considering my age, the gain is probably permanent. I went from a size-8 pant to size 12."

What about dress size?

"I don't wear dresses."

What? But why? They're so easy! That's why they're called "dresses." Put one on, and you're dressed. Girl, you're sixty! What're you waiting for? Okay, time to get a move on here.

I Get It

I work with many women through the American Cancer Society, and I've seen how it affects them. Breast cancer is uniquely devastating for each individual. Sadly, though, it has become commonplace in our society, and everyone knows someone who's been afflicted with this disease—and if they don't now, they almost inevitably will. One in eight American women will develop invasive breast cancer in her lifetime. From what I've seen, no matter how smooth the treatment and recovery, the disease is seriously damaging to a woman's sense of femininity and sexuality.

Though I haven't had cancer myself, I do know what it's like to have permanent scars. Mine have faded, but they're still visible, a reminder of what I've suffered. And scars are one thing. When body parts are removed, even if they're "replaced," it's a whole other level of adjustment. You don't just feel "not the same." You really *have* been changed.

There's a reason organizations like Look Good . . . Feel Better exist. LGFB ✳ offers makeup, hair, and wigs to raise self-esteem in cancer patients. Style for Hire, a company I founded to train stylists to work with private clients, partners with LGFB to give style advice to these patients and helped create the content for their first-ever national program. Dressing well and comfortably during and after a cancer battle may not be one's chief priority, but it can improve self-image and boost mood. And when you're recovering from the fight of your life, any advantage can make a profound impact.

A friend of mine proved to me just how true this principle was. I first met a woman I'll call Olive nearly twenty years ago. She was an up-and-coming graphic designer then, just starting out, and trying to get her designs featured in magazines. I was an assistant at *Vogue,* and introduced her to an art director and helped her get started.

✳ ***The Look Good . . . Feel Better*** mission statement: "LGFB is dedicated to improving the self-esteem and quality of life of people undergoing treatment for cancer. It is our aim to improve their self-esteem and appearance through complimentary group, individual and self-help beauty sessions that create a sense of support, confidence, courage and community." Wigs, hair, nails, makeup, color charts, they run the whole beauty makeover gamut, all for free for people with cancer. It's a great organization.

Okay, donation pitch over. But really, go donate.

(Olive went on to become a mega-success with her designs in major magazines. Can I pick 'em, or what?)

A gloriously slim, preppy blonde, Olive had always been the picture of sunshiny good looks and health. Cut to fifteen years later, or about three years ago. I went to a Christmas party at a friend's house and scanned the crowd for a familiar face. I noticed a woman looking at me, but I had trouble placing her.

She came up to me and said, "Hi, Stacy. It's Olive."

I simply couldn't comprehend what I was seeing. The formerly long-haired blonde had shaved her hair into a Mohawk, and was dressed completely in black leather, from her motorcycle jacket to her steel-tipped boots.

Dumbfounded, I asked, "What happened?"

And she told me. Not long before, she had been diagnosed with breast cancer. She'd had to have surgery. She didn't want to watch her hair fall out from chemotherapy, so she cut it off herself. She was told she'd never have children, so she froze her eggs. She had a boyfriend and put it to him: "Stay or don't, but you'll have to step up if you do." As it turned out, he did.

As amazed as I was by her physical transformation, what really impressed me was how Olive immediately took control of her life, as much as possible, in the face of illness and possible death. She did all the proactive things she could, and it radically changed her as a person. Obviously, she'd changed physically. But her presence—her new toughness—was an amazing display of beauty and bravery. It was the first time I realized that getting sick affects the way you see yourself, that your health can, in fact, affect your style, and that there are proactive choices. So much of one's feminine identity relies on feminine parts. How do you continue to feel feminine without them?

Not long after that night, I attended a fund-raiser for the American Cancer Society, and someone asked if I'd consider doing a free makeover on a woman who'd had a double mastectomy. She had been invited to speak at the Triple Negative breast cancer organization in New Jersey after being a go-to mama-bear source of information on their blog. Though she wanted to speak in person, she said she couldn't because "I have nothing to wear." In her case, it was true. After a double mastectomy and chemo, her body had changed significantly. I was happy to help her find an outfit that made her proud to stand in front of an audience, and have been helping other women with these issues whenever I can ever since then. Olive, in her head-to-toe black leather, continues to be my inspiration. During a weak time, she used style to strengthen her resolve. She was determined to own her image instead of letting cancer rob her of her identity.

Most people don't think twice about

style during an illness. Obviously, the last thing anyone needs to worry about is whether her hospital robe is the right shade for her coloring. (For the record, I have never seen a flattering hospital robe.) I'm certainly not suggesting that you should get out of bed while you're struggling with treatment. Style is the first thing to go when we're sick. But when you're ready, you can use style to feel better on the road to recovery as a *part* of recovery. It is one of the easier things to pick back up. Style is a source of strength when you feel weak. Wear cashmere and silk and cotton jerseys, which feel soft and gentle on your skin. Put on a bright color to feel vibrant. Rock a headscarf. With illness, you don't have control over your body, but working on your style can feel like taking a bit of that control back.

Style is often written off as superficial and not an essential part of life. The fact is, you *can* live without it. You don't need style to breathe. But, if you're up for it, style can have a greater purpose in your life than you might have ever imagined or intended. Style is about identity. And holding on to that, in the midst of illness, can be a real lifeboat.

No one can take life for granted. Janis certainly doesn't. At sixty, she is a survivor. She's been proactive about her treatment and recovery research. She's participating in survival causes, such as support groups and charity fund-raising events. And now she's put herself forward to be in this book, with the goal of integrating new artificial parts, feeling whole, and being an inspiration to other women.

Is she amazeballs, or what?

Janis's Start-over

THE SYMPTOMS:
Ill-fitting tops, and outfits with no sense of femininity

THE UNDERLYING CAUSE:
Cancer

THE PRESCRIPTION:
Using style to integrate a sense of femininity and sexuality during recovery

Women's relationship with our breasts is complicated enough when they're healthy. Since our first visit from the boob fairy as adolescents (thank you, Judy Blume, for *Are You There, God? It's Me, Margaret*), we've been examining them, finding both beauty and fault. We imagine them altered (bigger, smaller, perkier, higher, rounder, etc.), or actually have them augmented, reduced, or lifted. Packed with nerve endings, they're connected to our sexuality. Breasts are part of what it means to be a *girl*. Throw into the mix how our breasts are appraised by anyone who gets to see and touch them and every association becomes intense, personal, and emotionally loaded.

And then to learn that your breasts could kill you?

Almost three years ago Janis's breasts were removed, and refashioned. She thinks her new ones are fine, but they're not hers. The reality is,

they're artificial material. Fortunately, though, she can reclaim the feelings of femininity and attractiveness that cancer took away. Before her mastectomy and reconstruction, Janis's work-from-home casual everyday T-shirts-and-man-pants style didn't necessarily make her feel

The universally flattering V-neckline highlights the girls and keeps the neck open for a longer, leaner top half.

Janis has never tried animal prints or pencil skirts before. Well, there's a first time for everything. Experiment with bright, bold patterns or new silhouettes after an illness, or at any time. Always try new things, but not necessarily trendy ones. Instead, think modern and relevant.

pretty—but it didn't have to. Post–surgery and drug therapy, though, she could use a strong dose of feminine-infused style.

That doesn't necessarily mean that she has to go for a delicate or fragile look. After an illness, the more strength you can feel, the better. What I'd like for Janis is to visually connect feminine strength and style. So Janis has to pick up a few things:

DRESSES. Putting on a dress is the fastest way to feel feminine.

SKIRTS. Another girl-only garment (advisably anywhere, except in Scotland) and wardrobe staple. Janis can wear pencil skirts with heels and a silky top for a night out with her hubby, or with a sweater and flats for a lunch or meeting.

PATTERNS. I've said it before, I'll say it again: Patterns are an easy way to show your personality. Floral or animal prints say feminine in different accents.

HEELS. Six to sixty, putting on a pair of high heels will make you feel feminine.

JEWELRY. Janis wore a gold anklet to the shoot. I loved it. It says Jersey girl and the eighties, and I want it to make a comeback. I seriously want one, bad.

I don't believe in *only wearing* sentimental jewelry—things you never take off (except maybe your wedding ring). You should have a jewelry wardrobe just like a lingerie and clothing and shoe wardrobe, different styles to mix and match to create different vibes on lots of great basics.

A belt creates a defined waist and brings out feminine curves. A waist is the most important part of an hourglass figure!

LINGERIE. Some silky nightgowns, quality panties (not six for a dollar in packs), as well as new bras. Nothing says sexy like some sexy lingerie. Janis said she wasn't happy with the bra fitting she had after her reconstruction. So get another, pronto!

DETAILS. They don't have to be girly (like ruffles and big buttons). Just any extra points of interest that make a garment look empowering and feminine, like a strong shoulder or stitching, or nipped-in waist.

COLORS. Think vibrancy. Saturated colors that create contrast with your skin are a great mood lifter.

Mixing in menswear with more feminine pieces is also a great way to play with tough and tender femininity. Natural, breathable soft fibers like cotton, silk, and cashmere are good for recovery.

Why This Works

The idea is for Janis to feel grounded in her femininity and sexuality. She's not just a scrappy lady but also elegant and sophisticated. I didn't want her to feel as if she were wearing a costume but to inhabit both the clothes and her body comfortably.

• **THE DRESS:** My first objective was to get Janis into a dress. Not putting her in separates was intentional, as I didn't want her to feel as if her body were in separate pieces. A dress is *one* thing—like a onesie, but she's a little too old for that. (See? The truth stings.) We could have put her in a boilersuit, so she'd be ready to work under a car (she does sell airplane parts for a living!), but that wouldn't really promote the feminine vibe we're going for here.

I wanted to find something that felt age appropriate and not too frilly while still being feminine and vibrant. The neckline shows a little skin, and is a nice V-neck that isn't too deep or revealing, therefore preventing any self-consciousness. I chose a cobalt blue to complement and enhance her eyes. Also, the pleating at the chest flatters her shape without calling undue attention to it.

• **THE BELT:** Don't waste a waist! Defining Janis's just adds to the womanly silhouette. The red is in bright contrast to the blue—it's a deliberate signpost so you don't miss the waistline here.

• **THE JEWELRY:** The choices here are subtly filling in the negative space. Look for jewelry pieces that follow the neckline and cut of the clothing. A V-neck should have a pendant or a multitiered necklace that fills the V. A crew- or scoopneck needs rounded necklaces, like a bib. Wherever an outfit exposes skin (like a three-quarter sleeve, short sleeves, etc.), there is an opportunity to bejewel it.

• **THE SHOES:** Have some fun! Try a leopard-print shoe. This platform sandal isn't too high. A neutral print—like any solid-color neutral—can be worn with solid colors and adds visual interest if mixed with other prints, like a bright floral. And this is an easy, non-threatening way for Miss Janis to try an animal print without committing to an entire animal look *like a BOSS.*

Yes! ....And?

Accept the unvarnished truth and build your style strategy from there.

"I had cancer."

You can feel sorry or bitter. That's your right. Or you can be proactive and feel "blessed" like Janis. Illness, like style, is a question of perspective. Perspective involves choice: You have the option to be positive or negative. You can complain about what's happened to you and what you don't have, or take the very first lesson of "yes" and accept what's been given to you. You're in control of how anything that happens to you actually affects you. It's easy to say "Cancer is horrible"; it's harder to say "I had cancer, and now I'm going to do something good with it." Writing a letter to be included in a book about style was Janis's way of claiming the "yes" and living with the "and."

"My boobs are fake. They don't move."

Yes, you might have some trouble fitting tops. So strategize. Step one: Look for knits and stretch fabrics that allow for some give, including microfiber, cotton jersey, and ponte fabric jackets. Step two: Alter tops, dresses, and jackets to fit your body. If you've never done this before, welcome to the wonderful world of tailoring. It's amazing what can be accomplished with a needle and thread and someone who knows what to do with them! When buying clothes, fit the girls first, and then tailor the rest of the garment around them. You might have to go up a size in shirts and jackets. Resetting a shoulder to fit a chest can be an expensive alteration. Buy fewer, more versatile pieces and tailor each well to stretch your style dollar.

"I'm petite in a larger size on my bottom half."

If you're like Janis and on the border of plus and petite for your bottom half, finding pants may take a bit more work. The most important fit on a pant is the rise—the crotch. It must touch your anatomical crotch in order to be the correct fit. This is not a part of the trouser that can be altered. Many times petites who try to wear mainstream sizes will find the rise is too long, and a drop-crotched pant isn't the most feminine look. With petites, it's all about maximizing surface area. And because petites have less to work with, proportion is very important. Always define a waist. And curvy petites must be careful with the hem of skirts and dresses. Anything below the middle of knee will look matronly.

BRA NECESSITIES

Get a professional bra fitting. Eighty-five percent of women are wearing the wrong size—and a lot of them have been doing so for their entire lives. Do not go to a mass-market lingerie store for a fitting. Department store stylists or expert fitters at bra boutiques—I recommend Intimacy (store locator at www.myintimacy.com)—are worth going the extra mile for. Lifting the girls up where they should be allows us to see and utilize the waist they may have been invading. You always have to separate the boobs and the tummy, because the combination is a bummy. Bra fitting does not cover you for life. Even a five-pound loss or gain is reason enough for you to go in for another fitting.

GO FOR THE SOFT, THE BRIGHT, THE LIFE-AFFIRMING

Pamper yourself with the softest fabrics you can find to increase overall comfort. Try wearing bright jewel tone colors as they can add vibrancy to skin tone (and color is said to improve mood). Wear structured fabrics with more tailoring to camouflage weight gain and thicker, bulkier fabrics (like heavy knits) to camouflage weight loss. Wear anything and everything that affirms you and your fight and that makes you feel even a tiny bit better.

"*The thing that is really hard, and really amazing, is giving up being perfect and beginning the work of becoming yourself.*"

—ANNA QUINDLEN

SARAH C.

Dear Stacy:

Hello! I'm Sarah, 26, and recently relocated to New York City from Arkansas. After spending a summer here a few years ago and loving every minute, I knew I wanted to give New York a try for real at some point. The opportunity presented itself, so here I am. I'm waitressing at a lovely restaurant, baking, singing as often as possible, and window shopping.

I *love* clothes! Dresses and skirts, oh my, please and thank you! I have a fairly good idea of what shapes and proportions work for me, but I don't have a consistent style. My tendency is to be extremely picky *and* indecisive. Also, I'm hyper aware of how young I appear. I always struggle with what looks age appropriate and being unsure of what I actually like. I don't need to have a huge wardrobe. I definitely prefer to save for a smaller selection of quality pieces.

I am my own worst enemy when I shop. I can talk myself out of anything. It's ridiculous, really. Combine my neuroses with my very petite yet feminine frame—4'11"; 96 pounds; 32C bra—and most of my shopping ventures end with me empty-handed in frustration. I shop assuming I'll find nothing. Hate that. I need help finding a balance of youthful, fun, and mature, and building a versatile, interesting wardrobe. I have only one handbag, and most of my jewelry dates back to high school. I'm in a rut, and I want out.

Thanks,
Sarah C.

When Sarah

arrives at the studio, I'm bursting to tell her why I chose her for the book and what my insight was about her (more on that in a minute), just to see her reaction. I'm mentally prepared for her to deny it. But if she agrees? I'm totes ready to high-five her.

Before we start talking, I can tell by her smile that she's self-possessed. I also think that I could bench-press her. She is *really* petite. Her personality and cool reserve are a little intimidating to me at first. From a style perspective, Sarah isn't a total train wreck. Just . . . bland. I love her leopard-print ballet flats, but they are shot. The rest of her outfit—the faded jeans, shapeless beige sweater—is visual oatmeal, the no-sugar-added kind.

"I was in a status quo situation in Arkansas," she says. "No direction. I was finished with school and working, thinking about what was next. Then a friend called and said a room in his apartment in Manhattan opened up suddenly. This was in May. By July I moved here. I left a boyfriend back in Arkansas. We'd just started dating. He wants me to come back, but he knows that if I do, it'll have to be in my own time. He'd never move here. He hates New York. We're doing the long-distance thing for now."

I'm impressed. Long-distance relationships take serious commitment and hard work. If she left a good thing behind, I'm guessing she's pretty strong-minded.

"My educational background is in musical theater. I thought I'd pursue that in New York," she says. "But now that I'm here, I'm not sure it makes sense long term. Even if you have artistic tendencies, you can do it for yourself, and not make it your career. I'm afraid that if I do singing for a living, I'll lose the joy. People say, 'If you can picture yourself doing anything else than being a performer, you should.' I'm thinking it over while I enjoy the city and wait tables."

Is she auditioning anyway?

"I'm not. I know I came to New York to do that. I feel like I should audition. But I'm just not motivated to do it. I admit, the competition is intimidating. A lot of the singers have a dance background, too, and I don't. Besides, why expend that energy when I can be looking for something that's more inspiring? I've always enjoyed singing. But I feel like I've already done that. I earned my degree, and now I want to move on. I get bored easily. I need variety. I can't do the same thing every day or I'll go crazy. Lately, I've been enjoying cooking and food, working in different restaurants. I'm a vegan. Maybe I'll pursue that."

Based on the fact that she gets bored and wants variety, I'm surprised she's not more into fashion. I ask Sarah about her style choices.

"I'm not overly creative about what I wear," she concedes. "I don't know what I'm looking for, or what I like."

She doesn't know what she likes? That surprises me.

"I don't have a particular genre of clothing I gravitate toward. I do have a hard body to fit—small, but not boyish. I always need a lot of alterations. ✳ I go shopping with good intentions and quit because I'm intimidated and overwhelmed by the choices. I look for an outfit that feels right for me. But that doesn't happen a lot. I tend to shop where the clothes are simple, neat, and clean looking. I'd like to be forced out of my comfort zone, to be more adventurous and creative. I doubt myself a lot."

Sarah doesn't give me the impression of being ruled by fear, though. She seems quietly competent. She moved from Arkansas to New York on a whim. That's not how a fearful person behaves.

"I fear looking young," she says. "I have a general fear about being uncertain what the future holds for me. At this point, I don't have a clear picture what comes next."

I have no doubt Sarah will achieve what she wants to achieve—as long as she doesn't get in her own way. Her modus operandi right now is inaction due to indecision. She can't decide what to do with the rest of her life, or what to wear tomorrow morning. She can't silence the endless deliberations and pull the trigger.

I suspect that this is what's holding her

✳**Go the extra mile**: No size fits all. There are 7 billion (and counting) genetic variations of the human body. They simply can't all be expressed in standard clothing sizes. It would be nice if everyone on earth had a specific size for his or her unique shape. But size 0 to 7 billion is not going to happen. Standard sizes are an approximation of proportion. Just that. In order to fit your body, figure out which size comes closest, and then tailor your clothes to fit your own variation of shape.

back. In her letter, Sarah described herself as "particular" and "picky." Picky doesn't usually mean choosy. Picky often becomes an excuse to avoid having to make a choice. Why not make choices? *If she doesn't choose, she can't make a mistake. If she doesn't try, she can't fail.* Sarah came to New York to be a singer. Before going on a single audition, she decided she wasn't into it anymore. *If she can't be the best, why play the game at all?*

High five or denial coming up . . .

I share my perceptions about what's really holding her back, and brace for a slap.

"You're totally right," she agrees. "I have really high standards for myself, and if I think I can't do something perfectly, I just don't do it."

Ahhhhh . . . a fellow perfectionist. That's why I could read between the lines of her letter. We bond instantly (and we high-five!). Perfection is the enemy of style. It's actually the enemy of *all* life experiences. If you don't try, you don't fail—but you don't succeed, either.

I Get It

Where does my own drive come from? Hard to say. My sisters have it, too. My parents applied subtle pressure by being very talented and successful. I became aware of my tendency to stick only to those areas where I knew I could excel or that came easily to me—hence, my total avoidance of math and gym. I have no coordination (unless it involves clothing).

In classic perfectionist style, if I can't do something well, then I don't do it at all. This pretty much limits my overachievement to the only area I know I'm good at—the psychology of style and putting people into the right clothes for them. I don't venture outside my wheelhouse. Otherwise, I feel vulnerable.

I've dug into my comfort zone with both heels (high ones, natch). On the rare occasions I've left it, I was thrown out against my will—like getting dumped by boyfriends I should have broken up with myself. Why didn't I? I was paralyzed by the thought *What if this is as good as it gets?* (FYI: They weren't.)

I did the same thing with jobs. My final days at the late, great *Mademoiselle* magazine come to mind. I landed at that magazine for the second time in 1997, having already cycled in and out as an assistant a few years before, with the new, impressive title of Senior Fashion Editor. I thought it was the best job I would ever have. I hung my pride on the very title.

For all four years as SFE (wow, I'm just now seeing how the acronym for that title is "safe"; that's both prophetic and ironic), I loved the job, my boss, my colleagues, the work itself. But in my last year I was blindsided by a change at the top of the masthead. The incredible editor in chief who had hired me was fired. This happens often in the magazine business, and rolling with staff upheaval is essentially part of the job. You have to stay flexible to survive.

The new boss arrived, and from the start our sensibilities clashed. During her first week she called the entire fashion department of a dozen editors and assistants into the conference room for a meeting. She proceeded to go over every single page of the latest issue of the magazine to discuss what she liked and hated about it.

In that particular issue, there were three big fashion stories. She harshly criticized two of them—the two I'd worked on.

It was clear she favored a style other than what I'd been doing and what *had* been the magazine's aesthetic directive. There was no discussion of how the choices were made or how well they fit the magazine's former point of view. None of that mattered. No one defended my stories—not even me. And I had been so proud of them. The new boss had already decided her favorites—and I was *not* one of them.

Meeting concluded, the new boss invited the fashion department to go out for drinks that night. I was so shattered— maybe it was cowardly of me, or maybe it was a sign of emotional resignation—that I just couldn't go. On the subway ride home, I was sobbing so hard that a man sitting across from me handed me a tissue. A complete stranger took pity on me and lent me some support. Too bad he didn't work at the magazine.

The writing was clearly on the wall. And still I didn't leave. I was miserable, but I couldn't walk away from the job and title that seemed so important. I went back and forth in my mind—*should I stay or should I go?*—obsessively. Ultimately, the decision was made for me. I was fired within two months of the new editor's regime.

I hadn't been unemployed before but already had an agent to get freelance styling work in advertising. Being an untitled, unaffiliated freelancer with no guaranteed income played to my own worst fears of failure. I called lots of colleagues I'd helped during my tenure at the magazine, asked if they had any job leads or freelance work to throw my way. Not much turned up. After eight years in fashion editorial, I was suddenly in the terrifying position of having to start over from square one.

Square one put me on the path that led to where I am now. If I hadn't been fired,

I wouldn't have established myself outside fashion magazines, or started to work with real women of all ages and sizes. It was during this period that I began to sort out the crucial differences between fashion and style. I saw with my own eyes how profoundly style could impact real women's lives. Personally, I was happier, too. If I'd stayed in fashion editorial, I wouldn't have learned these important personal and professional lessons, all of which came to play when I got an out-of-the-blue call to go to the TV audition that changed my life. (P.S.: If you don't know the outcome of that story, I'm not sure why you're reading this book.)

The fact is, you never know what's going to happen next. People make plans or set career paths and life throws a curve ball at them. We believe getting dumped or fired is the worst thing that could happen, when in fact it could lead us to a life we couldn't possibly have imagined. (Where would Adele be if she hadn't had her "rubbish relationship?")

"Failing" takes you to unexpected places. The less fear we have of failing, the more open we are to the possibilities of the unknown. Style is a great way to practice taking chances. It's like putting on "risk" training wheels. With style, you can casually flirt with failure. You can even have a one-night stand with it, wake up the next day, and decide to swear off that outfit forever. You start again with a clean slate every single morning.

For someone like Sarah, who fears making a mistake, the most important thing she'll learn from me is that if you don't allow for the possibility of failure in style, you can't ever achieve success with it either. There is only exploration, and if you don't explore, you can't evolve. If you don't take a step, the path will never appear.

Sarah's Start-over

THE SYMPTOM:
Plain-Jane, blank-slate clothing that is devoid of true personality

THE UNDERLYING CAUSE:
Perfectionism

THE PRESCRIPTION:
Try and Buy

As a curvy petite, Sarah is a tricky fit. As a perfectionist with super-high standards, she's an even tougher sell. Sarah says she can talk herself out of anything. Ruminating about every decision is how perfectionism causes style stagnation.

She perceives style as being right or wrong, with no shading in between. But while there are technical rules, which anyone can learn, for how clothes fit and which colors are best for the individual, style is fundamentally about personal expression. That involves no right or wrong—only what feels authentic. Sarah's inner compass, though, is on the fritz. For fear of being wrong, she can't let herself gravitate toward anything in particular. Instead, she falls back on utilitarian basics, not even bothering with accessories. (*How* can anyone not *bother* with accessories? They should be a USDA food group!)

I find it fascinating that Sarah has the guts to move cross-country but that she's incapable of committing to a blouse.

To have presence, small-framed women should wear form-fitting clothes, like skinny jeans and pencil skirts. Wider-cut clothes look like you're drowning in them. In particular, pencil skirts say "sophisticated" and "mature" on someone like Sarah, who worries about looking young.

Look for interesting details (like piping) on classic pieces (like a white shirt) to give them a twist and add some sophistication. Be careful with pastels and primary colors. Wear them with modern cuts and accessories, or get "typecast." Leave pastels to grandmas and primary colors to grandkids. One "p"—for petite—is enough.

Sometimes the small risks, the day-to-day ones, are harder to implement than the one-fell-swoop, bold, big ones. If Sarah could think differently and pull herself out of her style rut, other parts of her life that seem stuck might be positively affected.

The risk = reward quotient of style is instantly accessible: You can see the difference with your own eyes as soon as you step in front of the mirror. In Sarah, I see a woman who needs a gentle shove out of her comfort zone.

She has to try. There's a reason it's called "trying on" an outfit. You're just sampling it—no major commitment, no signing on the dotted line in blood. Sarah's tendency is No Try, No Buy. But she's got to try on a lot of clothes to sharpen her instincts and develop her own style. Typically, I see a lot of women make the mistake of Buying Without Trying, and wind up with a closet full of clothes that don't fit and stay there with the tags on for years. Opposite problem, same result: nothing to wear.

Sarah has to expect to try, and try again. And it needs to be a concerted effort. Taking five pieces into the dressing room, hating them all, and walking out of the store doesn't count. For example, you may have to try on two dozen pairs of jeans to find the right pair that fits your body.

Heels with details like studding, crystals, and grommets look tougher than say a ballet flat, and work toward a more "take me seriously" look for petites.

Petites with long torsos should raise the visual waistline to make your legs look longer and balance your body proportion. A low waistline will make short legs seem even shorter. Go for a higher-rise trouser or a jean with a thicker waistline. No low-rise jeans or tunic sweaters.

Flats are totally acceptable for petites, especially flats with a leg-lengthening pointy toe. Also try fun color combinations to read as more fashion-forward.

When lightning does strike and Sarah finds a sparkly top or cute pants that work, she has got to take it to the register and buy it. Breaking news: If you buy a non-final sale outfit from a store that takes returns, bring it home, and decide later on that you hate it, return it and get your money back. Further, Sarah understands the importance of tailoring when you're a petite. You can easily buy an item, leave the tags on, take it to a tailor, see if any possible alteration is worthwhile and affordable, and if not, you can return that, too.

To break herself of the No Buy habit, Sarah should force herself to make a purchase every time she shops. Ideally she should buy whole outfits, working out what goes with them and accessorizing them while shopping so there are no decisions to be made later on when she attempts to get dressed. But if that feels overwhelming, she can walk before she runs, and make a small purchase: a scarf, a pair of earrings. Accessories like these will be the first steps toward making her boring basics a little bit more exciting, and will look as if she's made a definitive style choice. Eventually, making choices and purchases won't be so painful.

Why This Works

Sarah presents a real style challenge. It's very hard to get a petite with a long torso, shorter legs, and curves into proportion. Every item she's got on goes to creating some body balance.

• **THE TROUSER:** A thicker-banded waist raises her visual waistline and lengthens her leg. A printed pant is modern and sophisticated and keeps her out of the petite trap of looking too childish.

• **THE TANK:** I wanted to balance her top and bottom halves, so I used a black top with inset shoulders. The cut of the tank broadens her shoulder to balance with her hips.

• **THE JEWELRY:** The necklace draws the focus up toward her face and, like the tank, creates a broader impression on top.

• **THE BAG:** Not only does this color-block style stand out nicely against a printed trouser, the structure of this bag is more sophisticated and ladylike than a slouchy one, adding another dash of "grown-up" to Sarah's look.

• **THE SHOES:** The pointed toe lengthens the leg, even with a cropped hem. A rounded toe with a cropped pant would do the opposite and make her look shorter, not longer. The black tank paired with this shoe act as bookends for the printed pant. Yes, they match. I could have done a red shoe here, but frankly, it would have been overkill.

Overall, this look has a retro feel to it. This particular style isn't the only choice for Sarah. She can do lady-er, tough, or whatever. But this represents *a choice*, because she needs to make one. The idea was to experiment with a deliberate look, to force her to see herself in a new way. She looks sophisticated, sexy, and adult all at the same time.

Yes!............And?

Accept the unvarnished truth and build your style strategy from there.

"It's hard to find clothes in my size."

People think that petites or the thin have it easy. But the truth is, there aren't that many options for petites out there. Like plus-size women, they will always have to deal with fit issues. If you are a petite, finding clothes will be harder for you than if you were a mainstream size, but that doesn't mean you shouldn't try. When you walk into a department store and see a sea of merch, it can feel overwhelming. Knuckle down and start choosing clothes—a *lot* of clothes. See the exercise as building an encyclopedia of information about designers and cuts. When you do find clothes that flatter your figure, you won't have to work so hard the next time. Just go back to what works.

"I look really young."

Looking young can have its benefits, except when you're not being taken seriously. Style is the answer to that problem, not the thing to avoid. Wearing loose jeans and shapeless T-shirts won't garner the attention and respect you want. But clothes that fit close to the body and have tailored cuts and better fabrics will. Have a particular point of view.

"I can't make up my mind."

The beauty of style is that if you do make up your mind, it doesn't slam shut like a steel trap. It's not making a deal with the devil. You can change your mind, and wear many different styles. Experiment and explore. Wear whatever resonates with you. Assemble a collection of styles that defines the different facets of your personality. Today, it's rocker; tomorrow, it's spunky and retro. Rethink what style means. It's a world of options. But you do have to choose *something*.

TO "P" OR NOT TO "P"

Petite, just like plus, is a marginalized size. Only 25 percent of all clothing is available in a P. Petite is not simply about being super-skinny or short. It's about smaller proportions overall: The actual measurements from the shoulder to the chest, chest to waist, waist to hip, etc. are all smaller in petite sizes. It's not just about length but about the distance from one point to the other in various parts of the body. In other words, there is less surface area to work with on a petite body. (I failed algebra, not geometry.)

But similar to regular sizing, petite sizes are cookie-cutter generalizations of the proportions of petite bodies. Women under 5'4" are not the only ones who may benefit from petite sizing. Women with short torsos or high waists may find a better fit with P tops, no matter what their height is. Similarly, women with shorter legs may benefit from the shorter rise in P trousers.

Even if you're petite, you're not limited to labels that say "petites." The good news is that many designers cut based on smaller proportions to begin with. In general, the smallest cuts are Japanese and Italian. Try all of it to see what works best.

SIGNS YOU MAY NEED A PETITE SIZE WHEN YOU AREN'T PETITE

TOP:
- Breast darts fall too low on the torso.
- Shoulder straps sag.
- You find yourself constantly pulling up shoulder seams.

What can be altered from regular sizes:
- The length of sleeves and the hem of shirts and jackets can be tailored at minimal cost.
- Resetting the shoulder on a jacket, shirt, or coat to make the width smaller is possible but expensive.

What can't:
- It's impossible to raise chest or waist darts that are too low.

BOTTOM:
- The rise of pants is too low, even when the waistband is altered to be smaller.
- Pockets fall too low on the hip.

What can be altered from regular sizes:
- The hem of a skirt, dress, or straight-leg pant, at minimal cost.

What can't:
- The rise of a pant, and shape of a pant other than a straight leg. Boot- or flare-cut hemming shortens the pant from the knee to the ankle and distorts the entire shape of the leg.

"A mother is a person who, seeing there are only four pieces of pie for five people, promptly announces she never did care for pie."

—TENNEVA JORDAN

TANIA

Dear Stacy,

I'm a 39-year-old mother of two who has allowed herself to get lost in parenthood. I was a slim, fashionable teen and young adult. I was even part of my high school modeling club. But when I became a mother, my weight spiraled out of control—up to 217 pounds, a size 18W. I placed less and less emphasis on myself and my style, and flat-out stopped doing things I'd always enjoyed, like dancing.

My daughters are currently four and seven. I want to be a healthy and positive role model for them. I've recently started dancing again—Zumba, Afro-Caribbean, salsa—and I have lost some of my baby weight. I got down to 190. I have no idea what size I am now, because I'm still wearing my 18W jeans and baggy shirts. Along with getting healthier, I want to dress better. Time is a huge roadblock for me. Along with the kids and my husband (we've been happily married for eleven years), I work full-time as an office manager for a small, clean-tech venture capital firm in Manhattan.

I would like to continue on a healthier physical and emotional path for a better life in style. But I need some advice on how to do it!

Best regards,
Tania

When Tania and

I meet, I immediately notice her bright, happy smile. Then a brighter white light distracts my eye down to her feet. I notice her sneakers, because her jeans are *rolled up*. They are the brightest blinding white—the jazzercise wrestling variety. I throw up in my mouth a little bit. As my eyes travel back toward her face, I see that the jeans are three sizes too big. On top of them sits a black *shmatte* that I only know for certain is a top because she's wearing it on top. She's also wearing giant gold earrings that have no business being on this casual an outfit. I have to sit on my hands not to reach out and take them off.

Uh-oh. I just gave Tania the eye-scan that Anna Wintour once gave me in an elevator.

However, I can imagine her kids lighting up around her. She is warm and cuddly. Tania is exactly what I expected from her letter: a woman enthusiastic and sweet as hell who knows how to take care of others but is clueless about taking care of herself.

She looks really happy about getting a mommy's day off, but I can see how tired she is, too. She's been stretched in every direction and appears to be hanging by a thread. Her clothes hang on her as if they are wet.

"I turn forty this year," she says. "I'm nervous about it.✳ I definitely want to

✳*I spent all* my thirty-ninth year hysterical about turning forty. And then I woke up the morning of and thought: *This is awesome.* The first sunny day in a month—and I felt great. I spent 365 days worrying about this day. Why? As soon as I crossed that line, I felt at peace with it. I got some external reinforcement when *People* magazine asked me to be in their "sexy" issue as the forty-year-old. Embarrassed? Nervous? Nope. I was flattered and overjoyed. I felt for the first time like I was young enough to have fun and old enough to be wise. I would no longer make the stupid mistakes of my twenties. (Well, I'm certainly trying a lot harder not to.)

start the new decade with a new mind-set and wardrobe. I hate what's out there for me, though. Plus-size clothing is horrible. It's matronly, ugly stuff. I'm missing that feel-good feeling. I do have a sense of style. I know what I like. But I can't find it."

No wonder she has no idea what size she actually is. Her pants are so baggy she has to hold them up when she crosses the room. She does take some pride in that.

"In the last seven months, I've lost thirty pounds. Before that, my weight was up and down, with two pregnancies. My body has been changing so much, I haven't been able to keep track of my size."

I'd bet she knows her daughters' sizes to within an inch. They're probably beautifully outfitted with new clothes every season. I work with a lot of moms on *What Not to Wear*, and I can't tell you how many of them walk around in sacks and sweats while their children look impeccable.

"It's true," Tania admits. "Everything is for them now. My priorities are to pay the mortgage and raise my girls. Every penny I make goes to them. I'm not the top priority."

No big surprise: Tania's got the Mommy syndrome, when you define success by self-sacrifice, when everything in your life is about the kids. Your time is for them. Your dreams are for them. Your job is to earn money to support them. Your own desires and needs (and style) fly out the window.

"I hear myself think and say 'When . . .' a lot," she says. "When the kids are older, I'll make more time for myself. . . . When we have more money, I'll update my wardrobe. . . . When I have more time . . . When I lose more weight . . . I know it's unhealthy to live in 'one day' instead of today. But right now, I'm too busy to carve out time for myself."

A whole life can go by being too busy and waiting for "when." Living in the future means barely existing in the present. If you can't enjoy things now, when will you magically develop the tools to enjoy things in the future?

Tania also has to contend with the past. "I worry about my weight because of my family history. Growing up, my mom was obese," she tells me. "She was a single mom. We didn't have money for healthy food, and weren't active as a family. Against the odds, I was slim until college. Then I met my husband and stopped dancing for exercise. I've let myself go for quite a few years. During my pregnancies, and when the kids were babies, the weight really piled on. But I started taking Zumba classes and have lost weight. I really needed to do it—for myself and to be a role model for my girls. I want to teach them how to eat well and exercise."

I ask if her husband does his part to help Tania get to Zumba classes—or go shopping.

"He does! My husband is an excellent

partner and father," she says. "No Hispanic macho posturing for him. He's a very involved, hands-on dad. In the fourteen years since we met, I've gained about fifty pounds. He doesn't care. He's loving and supportive in every way. But going to Zumba still means two hours away from my kids, and I can't help feeling guilty." ✱

Shifting gears, I ask about her work life.

"I love my job!" she blurts. Huge smile.

Tania's demeanor is so lovely and cheery. It's just her clothes that look miserable.

"I'm an office manager. I have a new boss, whom I really admire. She has an incredible work ethic, and is a working mother as well. I love seeing a woman who takes her career seriously and can be a mom, too. It's inspiring."

A dedicated mom with an incredible work ethic? Tania is describing *herself,* and she doesn't even realize it. She *is* what she admires in her boss. I ask how she dresses for work.

"I wear black slacks and a black sweater, and black flats. Sometimes, I wear brown," she says. (Oooh, *crazy.*) "Recently, I went to a big meeting and made the extra effort. My boss and the owner of the company noticed, and complimented me. It felt so good. I want that to be the standard."

Clearly, the external approval from her boss was deeply felt. Effort brought reward. Tania went the extra mile and received kudos. So what was it she wore? A suit? Colorful separates with statement accessories?

"A black dress," she says.

Whoa. Way to take a fashion risk. Did it fit?

"Sort of . . . ," she admits.

This just gets better and better. She must notice the look on my face.

"I know, I know. That's why I'm here! I need help with fit and sizes—and a whole look. When I was younger, before the mortgage and the kids, I tried to be trendy and current. Being trendy isn't

✱ *Guilt.* As a Jew, I was born with a great capacity for it. Logically, though, guilt has to be the most useless emotion known to womankind. Taking time for oneself is essential for a mother, wife, woman, and human. No one will accuse you of selfishness or think that leaving the house for an exercise class means you don't care about your children's welfare. (And if someone did? What a miserable bitch she must be.) The "I'm last" mind-set makes it easy for moms to lose themselves. They don't even realize they're doing it. Most of the time they don't even realize they're last.

appropriate at my age." (Well, it's all about how you do it.) "I want to look pulled together for work, and not like the crazy mom at the PTA meeting in PJs. Also, I want my daughters to see me as a role model for being confident and comfortable in my skin. It's about health, not vanity. When I went back to dance class, my older daughter asked, 'Are you trying to lose your fluffy stomach?' (New favorite word: 'fluffy.') I tell them I want to get in shape."

Did her daughter also ask her if she was going to buy some new clothes to go with the new body? *

"I have to be careful about that. I don't want to spend too much. I can probably just get some things altered," she says.

I don't think so. The jeans she's wearing are so big, they'd have to be reconstructed from scratch. She'd be far better off just buying new ones.

"But . . . ," she begins to protest.

But . . . moms have to invest in themselves. I understand that nearly all of Tania's paycheck goes to the mortgage and kids. She's wary about spending a dime on herself. I wonder how long it's been since she bought a new outfit.

"Seven years," she confesses.

I'm shocked. I'm actually speechless (and we know how difficult *that* is). Seven years without anything for oneself? That's six years and 364 days too long. Since

✱ Tania is already a role model. She's doing it—the job, the family, getting in shape. Now she needs clothes that are a reflection of her self-respect. How we dress transmits messages, whether we like it or not. What message does "Mommy doesn't deserve new things" send? Would a good mom sit her daughter down and say, "When you grow up you should ignore yourself, and proudly cast aside your needs for everyone else's?" Moms can teach their children self-respect by looking the part.

the last time Tania shopped, she's had two kids, risen at work, and sustained an enviable marriage. Her life has been moving right along, and she needs a wardrobe that keeps up. Her wardrobe is, literally, so 2005. Tania needs to drag her mind-set and wardrobe out of "when" and into the here and now (which is the only place and time life is actually happening).

Tania has made smart decisions about the big things in life. She married an excellent man, has raised two beautiful daughters, and loves her job. She's getting healthy and fit. If she could add style to an already great life, that's gravy. I'd love to see her take her giving nature and start applying some of it to herself. It's nice that Tania enjoys supporting her boss. But with the right suit and enough ambition, Tania could *be* the boss.

I Get It

I have this conversation with some of my mom friends regularly:

ME: How are you?
HER: The kids are well. Thanks for asking.
ME: Glad to hear it. How are you?
HER: Better. Lucy had a breakthrough in chemistry. It's a big relief.
ME: Fab! And you?
HER: John got a raise. He's really excited about it.

And so on. A lot of moms define themselves through their family. This is as true now as it ever was. No matter how progressive a society we become, most women regard themselves as the primary caregivers of their children. It's a biological imperative.

Don't get me started on my rant about the fallout of feminism. (Too late.)

Okay, one of the goals of feminism was to widen the lens for women to see themselves as something besides mothers. That worked. We have female CEOs, birth control, and the "childless by choice" movement. Despite permission not to, though, women can't stop feeling the traditional responsibility for their kids. That's biological, and it won't go away—not that it should. My point is, once we were expected to be Supermoms only. But now we expect ourselves to be Superwomen in dozens of areas. We have to be nurturing, protective, macaroni-gluing moms, but we also have to be stars at work, perfect wives, best friends, gracious hosts, chefs, marathoners, sexual dynamos, and more. I'm exhausted just typing the list.

There's one interesting split between moms who think of themselves as selfish for having kids and for then hiring nannies to watch them, while they pursue their own careers, and the selfless ones, who quit their jobs and sacrifice their other dreams to stay home and raise them. I ascribe zero value judgment to selfish versus selfless. Who am I to judge? I've never had to choose. How each woman makes her choice depends on her. Regardless of whether she falls on one side of this fence or the other, she's somehow perceived by society (or by herself) to have "failed" in the other way.

There is a third option: not selfish or selfless, but *selfness*. Love and support your family like crazy—because you want to and need to—*and* define yourself in terms of yourself.

The path to selfness can include style. Style allows you to recenter on yourself—literally, by focusing on what you see. When you look in the mirror, do you see an accurate reflection of the woman you are and want to present to the world—including your own children? Consider the shift: Change from fulfilling your family's needs exclusively to fulfilling your family's *and* your own needs, inclusively.

Some people might think, *Easy for her to say. What does she know about it?*

True, I don't have a husband or kids. I've thrown myself into my career. But my job has put me into contact with hundreds of Mommy syndrome cases. Time and again I get this feedback from those women: When they take time for themselves they feel more powerful at home, at work, and in the world. When moms feel attractive and strong, everyone benefits. If they feel unattractive and ignored, no one does.

Unlike a family, my career doesn't cheer me on from the sidelines or throw me a surprise birthday party. My Wikipedia page doesn't cuddle me at night. No one greets me at the door when I come home from work by saying, "Good job, hon. You're the best. We love you." (FYI: I've been informed that this does not happen even in the most loving families. Whatever. I like my fantasy, and I'm sticking with it. Stay with my point.) I don't always have a context for measuring my value. I have to do that for myself and say, "Go, girl!" Sometimes it's more like I just want to give myself a noogie and say, "Just get on with it, you ol' bat!"

Not having kids was a choice I made. There was only one time in my life I was so in love that I wanted to make a person with that person. It's a huge feeling to love so deeply that you want to fuse a part of yourself with someone else. That's not co-ownership of a mortgage or writing a screenplay together. That's an altogether different proposition. And unless I feel that way again, I probably won't have children.

Writing that makes me a little sad.

Then again, the idea of coming home to a screaming baby makes me want to shoot myself in the face.

If I really wanted kids and a husband, I'd learn to balance my energies—and work only ten hours a day. I'm ignoring that potential part of my life and letting another take over. It's easy to get on a one-track life, to lose the balance. I'm on the other end of the spectrum, but Tania and I do have the same problem: Neither one of us is very good at self-care. Neither one of us—like all women—has it all. Tania, however, can make changes and take shortcuts to getting there. She can dress stylishly enough to pass for having it all. (I can't fake having kids, although my friends would be happy to lend me some of theirs.) I understand why style hasn't been a priority for her. But it's a luxury she *can* afford. In fact, for balance and self-respect, she can't afford *not* to.

Tania's Start-over

THE SYMPTOM:

A closet full of *seven-year-old* black (or brown) worn-out clothes that are oodles too big

THE UNDERLYING CAUSES:

A combination of Mommy syndrome (taking care of everyone but herself) and Living in the Future (thereby ignoring the present)

THE PRESCRIPTION:

Time-Sensitive Working Mom's Strategic Guide to Shopping

Moms are the glue that holds the family together. Fine. Be the glue. Just add style as the glitter on top. How you look and feel are connected, no matter how hard you might want to ignore this truth. Moms are so busy doing things for others, why don't they do something for themselves, too? Make the change *now*. Start doing it in the present.

Tania's clothes fit her life thirty pounds and seven years ago. Time to upgrade. She needs two things to turn her style around: (1) reassurance from an honest critic (ahem, me), and (2) a plan. She's highly efficient at home and at work. I look at her and think, without irony, *I don't know how she does it*. But at the moment, shopping feels like the one insurmountable hurdle—as it should, after seven years of style hibernation. She'll be happier with a plan of action. The agenda:

FRONT-LOAD TIME FOR STYLE. When updating a wardrobe, put in some time and effort now to reap rewards later. The first big time-chunk is a morning or afternoon closet clean out. For Tania, that means throwing away everything that doesn't fit her body or life *now*. To avoid the mommy infraction, she can involve her kids. Ask them, "Does this look good on me?" They'll have fun helping, and she'll feel good about getting rid of the old stuff. Remember: Old stuff that no longer works for you can be donated. Take the tax refund and put that money back into your closet with updated pieces.

MAKE A LIST. Just like when you go to the grocery store to get ingredients for a recipe, you shouldn't go shopping without a list of things you need to buy. The list should be comprehensive and include everything you'll need for work, weekend, events, parties, exercise. Keep adding to it as ideas come up, and check off items after you acquire them. (For Tania's Shopping List, see page 116.)

SHOP WISE. Shopping, like exercise, is successful when it's consistent. Shopping for an hour two times a week to check items off a list is better than trying

Essentials for Mom: stylish outerwear, including a leather jacket and a trench coat with feminine details. These are classic investment pieces. They never go out of style, ever, and can be reinvented with new purchases every season.

Fitted jackets: Look for details like seaming or stitching to wear with basic black for work or with jeans for a weekend "mom-on-the-go" style. (I hate that phrase. What mom isn't "on the go"?) I can't stress enough the importance of blazers for women who carry weight in their midsection—the plus-size or post-pregnancy or plain tummy body type. A structured blazer does the work your body can't by holding a nipped-in waist shape. Add a belt for additional waist emphasis.

to tackle the entire thing in one day. (Although Tania certainly deserves to take a mommy's shopping day off every once in a while, too.) With the list in hand, go to a store with an open mind. Maybe you thought you'd get a jacket there but the dresses and blouses look more appealing. Stick with anything you can check off the list. No waiting for "day of" shopping or scrambling to buy an outfit the day before a job interview.

Blouses: Colored blouses with feminine details like ruffles work with suits and jeans. For wash-and-wear convenience, microfiber and cotton jersey are great. Go for three-quarter sleeves if you are self-conscious about your arms, for a look that feels more feminine than full-length and less sporty than short sleeves.

You'll never find the perfect thing when rushing, and there's no time allotted for tailoring. Instead, try on a formal dress that catches your eye even if you don't have an event coming up. If it looks great, buy it, have it tailored, and you'll be ready when an invitation does arrive.

ORGANIZE. The worst thing is to have a closet of separates that you don't know how to put together. To prevent this you can either buy whole outfits when you're out shopping or buy separates and organize them in whole outfits when you get home. Either way, arrange clothes by outfit, head to toe, and hang them in the closet that way. Morning of: easy grab and go. It'll only take five minutes to get dressed, and then you're ready. Organize by category: work looks; weekend basics; evening; and exercise.

Visually compelling accessories, such as scarves, belts, and purses, are a great way to add color and interest to basics at work and on the weekend. They are also so easy. You just need one—not a mess of accessories—to put the cherry on the top of the sundae and give basic outfits some life and energy. Of course this looks like a mess. We were experimenting!

Get yourself a jersey dress you can roll up in a ball and leave on the floor for six months, pick it up and it'll still look great. It's the least time-consuming wardrobe item for a mom I can think of.

Why This Works

First of all, everything here is a wash-and-go. No need to carve out more time for trips to the dry cleaner.

This is an outfit Tania can wear to work and feel proud of. It's totally appropriate to take it apart piece by piece for dates with her husband and playdates with her kids. Versatility is always a money- and time-saver.

It took no more than three minutes for Tania to get dressed. I want to remind working moms: It takes the same amount of time to put on good clothes as bad clothes. Maybe you'll need a nanosecond longer to button a shirt or zip pants. That's time well spent, too. Elastic-waist pants are like a "frenemy." They give you permission to forget to remember yourself. They seem kind, but they're not. They give you permission to ignore your body—what it's doing and whether or not it's expanding. Elastic is an excuse.

• **THE JACKET:** My favorite thing about the jacket is the shape and the color. (Okay, that's two things.) It does exactly what we want it to do: With a small shoulder pad, it broadens her shoulder, which de-emphasizes her chest and midsection. It nips in at the waist, and the fabric itself has some stretch. Emerald green is one of my favorite jewel tones. Surprisingly, this color goes with many others and can be utilized in the same way Tania would normally fall back on black and brown.

• **THE SKIRT:** Navy is a great alternative neutral to black and brown. This skirt is straight and doesn't narrow at the knee, which would effectively widen her hips. The uniform width does not call attention to her hips and lengthens her body. ✱

• **THE BLOUSE:** The printed blouse ties the solid pieces in the outfit together, mixing the green, blue, and purple, and turns it into the piece that unifies the outfit.

• **THE BELT:** Yes, you can accent a waist, even with a fitted jacket, by belting it. I love that this one is an embossed leather (makes it look like snake, but cheaper than snake) in iridescent dark purple—visually interesting but versatile!

• **THE SHOES:** Okay, I know she's not going to wear them too much. But they are so chic and we chose the color based on the colors in the print of her blouse. She can leave them in the bottom drawer of her desk and put them on at work. Oops. Now you know where to find Tania's groovy shoes.

✱**Everyone I know** has an interesting relationship to navy. People have negative associations with it: school uniforms; gym uniforms; prison uniforms. Get over it. It is a great neutral to mix with bright color!

TANIA'S SHOPPING LIST

Jackets

A working woman's and a mom's staple. *Any* woman's ally. Look for a couple of neutral-colored or neutral-print blazers that will mix and match with both work and weekend wear. (FYI: A neutral print is a print that from far away looks like a solid; for example: glen plaid, windowpane, houndstooth, or pinstripe. Mix with bolder prints for unique style combinations that are still work appropriate.) A leather jacket does double duty as well, and looks polished. Denim jackets are great for banging around with the kids and can be worn with sundresses and casual pieces in warmer months and climates.

Trench coat

Colored or neutral. I love lightweight trenches that cinch at the waist and protect you from getting wet. Tailored ones with detail in darker colors can sometimes do double duty as an evening coat. Ding, ding! Time- and money-saver.

Jeans

At least three pairs of dark uniform-wash denim. Find a fit that you love and gives great ass. Buy two pair: hem one for flats and one for heels. Let the third pair be a wild card. Try something fun that feels modern or relevant—as long as it's flattering—like colored or waxed denim.

Skirts

Pencil skirts: great in a stretch fabric, such as a double knit or ponte. Will work with all jackets and is especially flattering with blouses that have waist definition or a peplum. A-line skirt: universally flattering to all body types because of its inherent shape. The waist looks small because the hem is wider. Look for one that has structure, not one that is flowy and drapy, without being too stiff or exaggerated in shape.

Suit

Ideally, a three-piece suit—a jacket, pants, and a skirt—is perfect. Wear as either a trouser suit or a skirt suit, or wear the pieces separately. Make sure to buy it in a neutral color, for versatility and longevity. Ding, ding! Another time- and money-saver.

Tops

Easy-care fabrics in colors and prints are the most time-efficient way to show your personality. Look for tops with interesting cuts or details that make them *look* like blouses but *feel* like T-shirts. You'll be surprised at how fancy a cotton jersey can look!

Dresses

Day dress: Get a jersey dress, too (okay, this one doesn't have to have a zipper), but it should define a waist and still be tailored.
Cocktail dress: Doesn't have to be black, but should be in any solid color, especially one that's flattering to your eye, skin, and hair colors. You can change the feel of the dress by changing the accessories, exactly as you would with a little black dress.

Wedges

A working mom's answer to high heels. They give you some height but with more stability than a traditional pump. Especially good for women with high arches.

Nonathletic sneakers

Leave the jazzercise cross trainers at home. Sneakers can be supercool and look great. Choose ones with interesting detail or color.

Bag

When time is the most important factor, one bag that can go everywhere is helpful. Look for one that's sleek and structured enough to carry to work and big enough to throw in all the kids' stuff: Convertible bags with longer straps that can be made shorter; neutral colors such as gray and stone instead of black and brown are light enough for four-season wear.

Scarf

One printed beautiful scarf can turn a T-shirt and jeans into a real "outfit."

Yes!..............And?

Accept the unvarnished truth and build your style strategy from there.

"It's all about the kids."

No, it isn't. You draw oxygen, too. I absolutely understand why moms put everything into their kids. Along with love and a protective instinct, moms see their kids as an extension of themselves. But *everything* that's representative of you should matter, not simply your children—your*self* as well. If you dress your children well, you should adhere to the same standard you set for them. Dressing well is something that affects them positively, and it is something you can do for yourself.

"I've got no time."

Make time. That's the only way around that problem. You are the master of your time, and only you say how to spend it—and how you waste it. If you really think about it, anyone can scrounge up two hours a week, or one whole day, to shop. Watch a few fewer hours of TV, and convince the husband to take the kids to the movies while you run into your favorite boutique.

"I don't want to spend a lot now if I'm going to lose more weight."

Even if you're losing steadily each week, you need clothes to wear in the interim. Thank God there are options that are inexpensive but still trendy, stylish, and practical. Look for mass-market brands that partner with awesome designers. You'll look current and modern without spending too much. Don't make the rookie mistake of buying clothes that would fit your goal weight. Take it from a veteran fluctuator like me: You may make it to your goal but not necessarily in the time you think you will. Don't waste money. Better to buy some inexpensive interim clothes that fit—and will be more flattering. Wait until you get to your goal weight, and allow your body to settle there, before you buy investment pieces, which will then really motivate you to stay there.

ANOTHER CHECKLIST

I started writing these style shortcuts for moms, but the truth is, they are for every woman I know!

1. **DO LOCK AND LOAD.** Keep the girls up and high. Good bras and good jackets that keep you "contained" are an easy way to look put together even if you feel you are hanging on by a thread.

2. **DON'T WASTE A WAIST.** A corollary of #1, really. Keep the girls high so there is enough surface area on your torso to DEFINE your waist, whether you have a tummy or not.

3. **DON'T BUY THINGS WITHOUT TRYING THEM ON.** You are strapped for time as it is. If you get home and it doesn't fit, now you have to find a time to go back and return it. Or you won't. And then that item will sit in your closet silently taunting you that you wasted money and don't know how to dress.

4. **DO RECOGNIZE THERE'S A REASON IT'S ON SALE.** A corollary of #3. Don't buy things just because they are on sale. Just because an item has been reduced from a kajillion dollars to forty-five doesn't mean that your money is well spent. Ask yourself if it fits the utility and/or joy criteria: Does it fit well? Is it a piece that works into your existing wardrobe? Is it something you've been actively looking for? OR do you just look so smoking hot and happy that the piece needs to come home with you to remind you how much you DESERVE to feel this way? If the item doesn't do ANY or ONE of these things, then the fact that it is on sale makes about as much difference as what antiperspirant you use. They all smell nice, but do any really stop you from sweating? Maybe it's just me.

5. **DO BUY OUTFITS INSTEAD OF PIECES.** You save oodles of time if you already know you have a whole outfit to wear instead of buying a piece, getting it home, and realizing it goes with *nothing you own*. If you must buy one piece, make sure it works with at least two other items in your closet, or—just like that awesome "sale" item—it will hang in your closet unused, silently mocking you.

6. **DO MAINTAIN A BALANCED WARDROBE.** Just like good nutrition, balance is important in your closet. Think of a pie chart divided into quarters: neutrals, solid colors, prints, and textures. If you maintain this kind of division in your wardrobe, you will always have new and interesting combinations of outfits to try. It's worth noting that whatever you have the *least* of in your closet is the thing you probably need *more* of, be it pants, prints, whatever.

7. **DON'T WEAR WHAT DOESN'T FIT.** This should be obvious but clearly isn't. If you've lost or gained weight, do not wear clothes that fit you before. There is no easier way to look like you are a mess than to dress like you're a mess.

"*The great thing about getting older is that you don't lose all the other ages you've been.*"

—MADELEINE L'ENGLE

JUNE

Dear Stacy,

I just turned 57 years old. I work in high tech in Silicon Valley and have all my life (for companies including Apple and Cisco) as a marketing manager. Now that I'm rounding the bend towards 60 (OMG!), I find it difficult to dress well because:

1. Clothes in shops are designed for younger women. When I put them on, I just look older.

2. My self-image is younger than reality. I gravitate to styles that fit my emotional age but are ridiculously young for a gray-haired veteran.

3. I work in a youthful business. I'm typically the oldest person at the office. I don't want to be confused for anyone's mom. It's hard to figure out what to wear that'll be fashionable, not frumpy.

4. In Silicon Valley, suits are fashion "don'ts." You must look stylish, but not formal. That's tougher to achieve as you get older.

5. My job is to market cool, high-tech stuff. How does a fifty-something achieve a polished, "youthful" image as a marketer?

Needless to say, my figure, skin, and hair are not what they used to be. Yet trying to hide the aging just seems to add years, and looks like a cheap disguise. I know my situation is far from unique. There are many women who, as baby boomers, are in my situation. We have no choice but to shop in stores that cater to younger women. We work in companies where youth and a youthful look are prized. How do we overcome these challenges, and express who we really are through our images, and use it to help us continue to build on our careers?

With respect and awe for your ability to transform people from the inside out,

June

June

arrives at the shoot with two friends and a suitcase full of clothes she wants to discuss with me, item by item. My initial read on her is "very Silicon Valley," that characteristic mix of money and hippie. From her letter I know she's worked at Apple, and I preemptively associated her with Steve Jobs, the barefoot billionaire. (I am kind of obsessed with Steve Jobs . . . but that's another story.) In person, June is sweetly loopy *and* supersmart. She has lots of questions, the hallmark of a hungry mind. It's clear she's come to learn. June exudes happiness, like lots of the other women in this book. She talks about her husband and their son—a college freshman and fencer—and about loving Silicon Valley.

I have two words for her appearance: "shock and awe" (okay, technically that's three words). I'm shocked by her tapered mom jeans, loafers, and *two* shades of orange cardigans (as if it's easy to wear *one* shade of orange). Her hair is even worse in person than I feared from the photo she sent—a mullet. My awe is over her bright blue eyes, the *color* of her hair (which is a stunning platinum), and her perfectly proportioned, athletic body. (I'm not surprised when she later says she's on a swim team.)

"I'm a big fan, but I get frustrated that I haven't seen you work with many women my age," June tells me. "We need style help, too. As I've gotten older, it gets harder and harder to find clothes for women over forty. The problem isn't fit. I can wear regular sizes. The problem is age appropriateness."

She's right. Fashion seldom speaks to women over forty. When you reach a certain age it feels as if you might as well disappear, as far as most trends are concerned.

"It's frustrating, because I want to look good. What I wear communicates who I am and lets me make a statement about myself," June says. "I've worked hard for a long time. I have an expendable income. I could literally buy anything. * But there's nothing for me! As a marketing expert, it's fascinating how disconnected designers are from this demographic. The number of people who are about to retire is huge. A lot of boomers have money to spend. And yet boutiques everywhere are stuffed with clothes for the very young.

"Recently my friend and I went into a store because of the cute clothes in the window. We tried them on, came out of the dressing room to show each other, and burst out laughing. What the hell were we thinking? We looked idiotic. It was funny, at first. Then, not really at all. Cute in the window doesn't mean cute on a fifty-seven-year-old."

Window shopping is a letdown for most of us, actually. But June is right: Age makes it harder. You can't browse the same styles you wore ten years ago. We know we're going to change as we get older. It's important to understand style in a similar way—as an evolution.

"Where is the stuff for me?" she asks. "You can find frumpy clothes, for sure. But where's the chic stuff? It's frustrating! We live in a youth-obsessed culture—on TV, in movies, and in stores. As an older person, you really feel excluded. We're currently living in a country and culture of denial. Our population is getting older. One day, it'll happen to all of us. And when it does, let me tell you, you won't want to feel excluded."

Here's another youth-oriented industry: technology.

"Silicon Valley dress is pretty young and informal," June explains. "But we're not slobs. Well, maybe the engineers. The business-side people like me have to look fashionable. Not by New York standards, but I do need to dress more formally. I just joined this financial-engine firm as the VP of marketing. I'm advising people how to plan for a good life when they retire. My new job involves traveling. I'm intimidated by what to wear when I visit places like Boston. I don't really own any suits. I don't know how to shop for one. I want to make a good impression on clients from the East Coast. I'm baffled by what to do."

How about in Palo Alto?

"I've worked in Silicon Valley for decades, so I'm confident at work. But I'm the oldest woman in my office, surrounded by much younger women. They're cute and thin and wear cute clothes. I feel like their mother."

*June is a woman** who has money. In her case, I'd say, spend it. What she pays for on the price tag, she'll save in time and aggravation. For June it's not an issue of price. High-designer pieces inherently are high quality—the fabrics and the tailoring. That's why they're expensive.

But that doesn't mean you can't get older and look good *without* spending tons of money. *Spend the most you can afford*, but only what is within your budget. And tailoring anything inexpensive instantly makes it look like it was made for you.

If she doesn't want to feel like their mother, she shouldn't wear mom jeans and *two* cardigans!

"I used to be the cute young woman in the office. I feel like I've lost my feminine charm. Who's going to think the old lady with the gray hair is charming?" she asks. "I've been with my husband for thirty years, and am happily married. But I miss feeling feminine and attractive. I don't want to lose that, but I don't want to embarrass myself, either."

I appreciate June's candor. I don't think that, as they age, women talk enough about that nostalgia for being cute and young, for feeling feminine and attractive, and about how hard that transition can feel. It occurs to me that June deserves a style that speaks to her own frank self-awareness. Not an intimidating style. Not a cute style. But one that commands something new . . . like reverence.

"Part of the problem," June says, "is that I don't feel old. In my head, I'm thirty. I don't know how to dress for my age, and I don't know how to *be* my age. It's hard to bring the image in the mirror and the internal feeling together. I look one way and feel a different way." *

"All of these issues have really come to a head recently," June continues. "Five years ago my husband—a thin, fit, nonsmoker—had a heart attack. We were close to Stanford Hospital, and we got there in time to save his life. The doctors couldn't find a reason for the heart attack. They called it a fluke. One month later my brother called and said he needed a kidney transplant. So I gave him one of mine. This all happened within a year— my husband's heart attack, my brother's close call, and my donating a kidney. All at once it seemed like I was only going through these life-and-death experiences. It changed my outlook and my priorities. What's important is feeling healthy and vital, being active and involved in life. I want to do more things, live richly and take advantage of what I can. I'm cognizant that I won't live forever. For

I have to laugh at that. I feel like I'm twelve years old, and often think, *When I grow up . . .* Then I see a photograph of myself, and realize, *Holy crap. I am grown up.* The gap between chronological age and emotional age is a real preoccupation for me. As a kid, I felt old. As an adult, I feel like a kid. We joke around that being a kid means feeling carefree. My childhood was far from that. As an adult, I've had my share of grown-up problems. But inside, a little kid wants to go out and play. I get really excited about chocolate. I love animals (especially weird-looking ones) and as previously noted, anything shiny and sparkly.

the years I have left, I want to surround myself with beauty—at home, on my travels—and to live in style in what I wear every day.

"I'm completely open to a new way of dressing," she says. "I don't even know what that look might be. I hope to find a balance between chic and age appropriate. I feel like I'm pretty hip and with it for my age. I don't know how to dress like it."

My first tip: To be "with it," don't say "with it."

I Get It

Aging is the ultimate paradox. We all hope to live a long life, but none of us wants to get older. Our society is obsessed with youth, beauty, and wealth—and wealth, if you have it, can buy you youth and beauty (well, vaguely). An incredibly successful friend of mine, a marathoner and a boss lady in her fifties, once said, "I'm not getting Botox or a face-lift. As you age you can look old, or you can look weird. I'd rather look old."

How sad that those are our choices. And how sad that so many of us actually opt for weird.

There is another option, and one I hope to make work for June: to look her age, and be proud of what that signifies. If we're lucky, we'll be showing our age for a very long time. The sooner we can feel comfortable with it, the better.

A few years back I was a regular speaker at the O You! Conference, Oprah Winfrey's annual inspirational speakerpalooza. In 2008 I was fortunate to hear the author and spiritual adviser Marianne Williamson discuss her book, *The Age of Miracles: Embracing the New Midlife.* She made the point that the human life span used to be something like thirty years. Now that our life span is expanding, the question women should be asking themselves is not what we should do at the end of our lives, but what we can do with the extra decades in the middle.

This idea knocked me off my feet. We spend a lot of time worrying about how we'll die, and fearing the time right before death—when we're so old and infirm that someone has to wipe the drool off our chin every two minutes. (Thought I'd paint that pretty picture for you. You're welcome.) Let's face it: When you hit that stage, style isn't a major concern. But between forty and death, you might have decades left to live, and you might want to live them with style.

Let's just say that the defining line of middle age for women, for all intents and purposes, is when they are no longer able to have kids. I mean biologically speaking, it's ideal to have a baby at nineteen. Three quarters of American babies are born to women in their twenties to midthirties. Once you cross thirty-five, the numbers drop sharply. Over forty? Precipitously. Even with incredible advances in fertility treatments, the majority of women hit the baby-making wall at forty-five (although there are rare exceptions). But when they are no longer reproductively useful, I feel like a lot of women hit an emotional wall, too. The biological imperative to be attractive to lure a potential mate is rendered functionally useless. (Yes, I said something way fancy and smart.) We look in the mirror and start to see how far away we are from the sandbox of youth—and how close we are to the mud of the cemetery. (Total Debbie Downer thought—just stay with me.)

I am definitely not saying that women must have (or crave) a baby to feel whole. Even a post-post-post-feminist workaholic in her early forties like me feels compelled to measure her value to society, and her attractiveness. The fact is, our culture does not appreciate the beauty of crow's-feet and liver spots on women. If you—by *you*, I mean *me*—don't have kids, aren't married, and are only sort-of dating, it's possible you'll be passed over for someone with a higher biological value quotient. Someone younger. (That bitch.) I'm kidding. Okay, I'm not.

In the best-case scenario, the older we get the clearer we come to understand that our sense of self should not be derived solely from our attractiveness. Pity the middle-aged woman whose entire identity and self-worth are wrapped up in trying to be a teenage beauty queen. I'm not suggesting that we should give up or let go of wanting to feel attractive. There isn't an expiration date on that desire, or the ability to accomplish it. Women can take that particular kind of pride in themselves at any age. It does require a shift in thinking, though. June spoke directly to the point when she spoke about her waning "feminine charms." She no longer felt like one of the cute girls in the office. And "cute," as we age—well, it's not cute.

"Cute" is flimsy and shallow compared to the gravitas of reverence. When you're young you can get by on cuteness alone. But, as we all know, cute is temporary. It's great while it lasts, but the day will come in every woman's life when whispery white minidresses simply look stupid. No, I'm not bitter. Just making a point. Reverential allure comes from a woman's power, wisdom, and experience. It's about knowing who she is and what she's capable of. When women recognize and radiate the knowledge of their own value, others will appreciate it and feel drawn to it. Forget cute—try elegant.

By the time you reach middle age you've amassed a lot of different skills. Feeling attractive as you age is another skill to add to that long list. You are allowed to feel pretty, or handsome, or whatever word you think is groovy (hint: Think it, but don't say "groovy" out loud). There *is* a beauty in wrinkles and liver spots. It is not the same beauty we equate with youth, but just like scars, they can be badges of honor.

Personal evolution amazes me. When my grandmother Mary died last year at ninety-nine, her face was still stunning. Being Sicilian, she had great skin, and she had silver hair down to the middle of her back, which she wore in a bun until her very last breath. She had been beautiful as long as I knew her. And my goal is to age like that. Mary got it: She wore her years proudly. All of us can do this.

June's Start-over

THE SYMPTOMS:
Frumpy sweaters, mom jeans, mullet

THE UNDERLYING CAUSES:
Facing age, frustration with fewer shopping options for women her age, mourning the end of cute

THE PRESCRIPTION:
New A.G.E. style

June represents an entire demographic of women who have the benefit of life experience but don't know how to dress to impress. They want to communicate who they are, and to express themselves

Show your A.G.E. in a statement coat, in patterns and/or black–and–white. Strong contrasts in general make bolder statements.

Look for shoes with some visual interest, be it embellishments, color, or shape. Keep them situation-appropriate: Remember, the office and the opera are not the same. Choose shoes that feel like art, bring you joy, and elevate the style of an outfit.

through fashion, but because there are so few trends that speak to them, they find it difficult to pull it off. Despite the challenges, it's not impossible to be the coolest woman in the office over age forty-five and beyond. Even in Silicon Valley, a young male's domain, a chic, mature woman can make colleagues of both genders sit up and take note.

The objective is to access a richer, deeper sense of femininity and powerful sexuality with style. This can be achieved because of, not despite, age. After forty you hit the New A.G.E. (Attractiveness, Generosity, and Experience) of style.

ATTRACTIVENESS. Cute is fine, for a puppy. When you're older, the vocabulary

of attractiveness is elevated and expanded. Who doesn't prefer words like "elegant," "sophisticated," and "chic" to that *other* c-word? (It's "comfortable," peeps. Get your mind out of the gutter.)

GENEROSITY. Be generous with yourself, not only with your family and friends. June has the resources to buy the finest fabrics and expensively tailored clothes. She can spend, and should invest in herself. At fifty-seven, having shipped a kid off to college and kicked ass at work for thirty-five years, June needs to say, "I can afford it, and I deserve it."

EXPERIENCE. Experience is power. And power is alluring. The feminine version of power dressing—bold-patterned

Silver foxes can wear silver! Paillettes (fancy word for sequins) look great for evening or paired with a suit to get a little shine for day.

coats, monochromatic outfits, statement jewelry, killer tailoring—transmits the bone-deep confidence that you can wear whatever you damn well please. It's simply not possible to pull that off unless you have years of wisdom and experience backing you up. June has got that, and a great sense of humor, and warmth, and a slammin' swimmer's body, which she needs to show off.

Menswear can give you a chic mix of strong and soft, but be careful about cuts, fabrics, and colors that look too masculine. Look for suiting with razor-sharp hourglass cuts to keep it squarely in the elegant and sultry category.

Why This Works

I wanted to start with a great fabric that looked rich and expensive. And then, a majestic color that contrasted with June's own coloring to create a look that demanded reverence.

• **THE SUIT:** Velvet! Yes, you can wear velvet without looking like a throwback. Velvet is so tactile. You want to reach out, rub June, and make a wish! (How I wish *I* look this good at her age!) This suit doesn't feel too formal for Silicon Valley. We're putting her lean, athletic frame to good use with clean, strong lines, masculine suiting, in a soft, feminine fabric and rich merlot color (which is a universally flattering color, by the way). This suit is a great day-to-evening option. Pair it with a brogue or loafer for day and a high heel for evening. The jacket and pants can be broken up as well for more casual looks. When June walked in with man-jeans and a double dose of cardigan, she was a raw slab of marble. In this suit? She's the carved statue.

• **THE BLOUSE:** I didn't put her in a button-up shirt, because she's not an eighties Wall Street exec. The pale coral silk ruffle shell softens it up, and adds femininity. She can also wear this for day with bright-colored separates. Another favorite color combo of mine: this pale coral with forest green.

• **THE SHOES:** Pale metallic snakeskin, high heel platform with a peep toe. If June were shorter or carried her weight in her bottom half, I might have gone with a darker shoe to keep her leg line long. Here the lighter shoe helps to balance the light, airy quality of her blouse. Snakeskin just says "expensive." It adds some visual interest, and this shoe style is timeless and versatile.

• **THE JEWELRY:** Make a statement. I chose vibrant green accents to contrast the color of the suit. The modern Maltese cross pendant complements but doesn't compete with the ruffled blouse. And the big bold rings are a standout against the outfit. Who doesn't love a little cha cha?

• **THE HAIR:** Looking at this haircut, it's hard to believe that June ever had her previous one. Short hair is one of those funny things: Some women think you must cut your long hair after forty. Some women think they should keep their hair longer to hold on to that sense of femininity and youth. I say, do what works, and this cut gives June such power, such beauty, frames her face, and takes advantage of the impact of her natural color.

Yes!............And?

Accept the unvarnished truth and build your style strategy from there.

"I'm fifty-seven."

Stop being mad about aging. There's no point. What are you going to do about it? Commission a portrait that gets old while you don't? (I can tell you, that story does not end well.) Look at every stage of life as an opportunity to reinvent your style, and as its own unique opportunity, period. It's a new reason to get busy with yourself. You may no longer be the cute girl, but get to know this kickass woman, now. She's got something new to offer you and those around her—just as she did in her twenties, thirties, forties, etc.

"I'm not cute anymore."

You haven't been, for a long, long time by now. Cute isn't cute after twelve. Cute is for fat babies and zooborns. (Shout-out to zooborns.com; adorbs baby animals daily!) You are not cute, no. But you're many other—amazing—things. It's a bad idea to define yourself by what you're not, anyway. So these are your options: Either be "not cute" or be elegant, sophisticated, chic, stylish, sexy, and strong. Hmmm. Tough call? Oh, please . . .

"I can't find cool age-appropriate clothes."

This is a weird thing to hear someone say. Can't find any clothes? I'm not denying that some have to look harder than others because of their age or size. But when someone says "I can't find clothes for me," nine times out of ten it means they don't know where to look. It's about cut and fit. When you wear clothes that are the right cut for your frame, when you understand your body type, you can find cool, age- (or size-) appropriate clothes anywhere. It isn't that designers don't want older women wearing their clothes. It's that no one instructs older women *how* to wear them. In general, the *quality* of the garment is essential, as is tailoring to your frame. *Less skin* is required. Less super-bright primary colors and more warm, rich tones. More texture and pattern and shine and bold accessories are your pals. There is no denying age, so let's engage with it.

BAD VINTAGE

Sweaters with bunnies on them are only cool if you're twenty, wear big bug-eye glasses, and live in Brooklyn, Portland, or Madison. For women over fifty, certain pieces scream "old" and should be avoided at all costs.

DON'T wear retro too literally. It'll look like you are old enough to have owned the stuff when the trend came around the first time. In particular, watch out for any dress with a petticoat or Peter Pan collar. That also goes for aprons, poodle skirts, bobby socks, seventies bell-bottom trousers, and polyester maxi suits. It's not groovy, baby.

DON'T match your accessories. No pearl earrings with pearl necklaces. No matching shoes to bag or hat to gloves. Watch out for hats and gloves, period. As you age, they should be used for utilitarian warmth value—unless you're going for an Auntie Mame–style status. Hey, I don't make the rules. . . . Actually, I do. Don't hate the player. Hate the game.

DON'T wear suntan hose. No knee hose of any color. The only exception to this rule is compression socks, but only under pants when you're on a plane (and don't tell anybody).

WATCH OUT for black and white. Extremes of the color spectrum look harsher during the day on skin as it ages (although print can sometimes alleviate that, like with that awesome coat June tried on).

STAY AWAY from super-high platform heels, commonly known as the stripper shoe. Because if you fall down, you won't be able to get back up.

STAY AWAY from hairstyles that require too much hair spray or too many bobby pins. If your hair doesn't move, you'll scare small children. Wear a hairnet only if you work in a school cafeteria.

PLEASE DON'T carry seven different wallets in your purse. You only need one. If you carry a change purse, photo sleeve, and credit card holder as well as a wallet, you should lighten the load, Grandma. My own grandma Mary had barely any wrinkles but a lot of wallets. It didn't dawn on her that the robber would take the whole purse and not just her billfold of ones.

"You can either hold yourself up to the unrealistic standards of others or ignore them and concentrate on being happy with yourself as you are."

—JEPH JACQUES

SARAH M.

Dear Stacy:

My name is Sarah. I'm a 26-year-old newlywed from North Carolina. I come from a large family of women. I have three sisters plus my mom. Out of the five of us, four are over 5'10". Because of my height—5'11"—I have the worst time finding pants that are long enough for me. I've tried ordering pants in extra long from websites. They arrive, and don't fit, so I have to send them back for another pair that arrives and doesn't fit . . . ugh. It can take me months to get one pair of jeans. Adding to that dilemma, I also have curves. I've got big ol' hips, and they aren't going anywhere.

Right now, I'm working part-time at a day care center, but I'm also going back to grad school for my master's in teaching. I need to look professional, especially when I start going on job interviews. But shopping for dress pants is a *nightmare*. They show every wrinkle, bulge, and pucker. If they're long enough, they're too tight in the hips. If they fit my hips, they're too short. It's like all clothing stores think tall women are beanpoles and only short women have hips. It's insane! I need help. Please.

Thank you so much,
Sarah M.

I'm excited and impressed that Sarah comes to the shoot wearing a blazer and dark-wash jeans. She looks pretty good, actually. Apart from that, though, I'm not getting a read on her. She's perfectly chatty. She's only twenty-six, but she carries herself like she's older. She doesn't seem particularly excited to be here—or unexcited, for that matter. She's very pretty, with gorgeous skin, clear blue eyes. When she does smile, I see she has *perfect* teeth.

When we get into her story, though, it's like the first thirty seconds after jumping out of an airplane: I feel the sudden, intense gravity of her self-deprecation. She comes off as defensive and a bit hard, and I recognize the affect immediately: physical self-consciousness.

She *is* tall. She has hips and very narrow shoulders. I feel it's important to acknowledge her unspoken vulnerability, and the actual challenges her body presents, and to *take care* with both. I want her to have a good experience. That means finding clothes that fit, balancing her body disproportion, making her feel attractive, and getting her to stop disparaging her shape.

"People have always reacted to my height and commented on it," she says. "It's normal in my family, so I don't really think about it until I look at a photo of me standing next to normal-height people. It hits me, and I think, *Wow, I am a lot taller.* I don't remember feeling self-conscious about my height as a kid. But, looking back, my mom did tell me to stand up straight a lot. Maybe I was subconsciously slouching."

But is self-consciousness a major factor now?

"It's a recent development," she admits. "I always kind of liked my body in high school and college, when I was tall *and* thin. I was 5'11" and 130 pounds through most of college. But then, about five years ago, I started to get hips. My size went up and up, and my feelings changed. To wear clothes you have to be tall and thin or short and curvy. I'm tall *and* curvy. Big hips. Love handles. I feel like a giant.

Okay, you *can* be tall, short, thin, curvy, in any combination, and still find flattering clothes for your frame. I'm not saying it's easy. But it is always possible. A defeatist attitude will not do anyone any favors, though. Assuming you'll fail will only make it harder to deal with your style challenges.

"I'm so self-conscious of my lower body that I haven't let anyone take a full-length picture of me in years," she continues. "On vacations and holidays, I make a point of saying, 'Only from the waist up!'"

What?! Even at her wedding last year?

"The wedding was different," she explains. "I had on a big ball gown with a full skirt. I felt covered up. So there were full-length pictures of me. The honeymoon was a different story. We went on a cruise to the Bahamas for a week. I was usually behind the camera taking pictures of my husband. He tried to take some pictures of me, and I made sure they were from the waist up. If any pictures did show my whole body, I deleted them." Huh. Well, that seems well played. *

Considering how self-conscious she is, it's ballsy of Sarah to want to be involved in this project. Pushing yourself to do anything you fear gets major points in my book. (And by that I mean both this book and my metaphorical "book.")

"The predominant emotion I have when shopping is embarrassment. I can't find anything that fits. My husband likes me in dresses. I can't really wear them to work at the day care center. Dress length is a problem, too. If they're above the knee, they're too short. If I bend over . . . yeah, the children don't want to see that. I need trousers to wear to work, but they're all wrong, too. They pucker, get wrinkles. If I find a pair that does fit my hips, they'll be too short. I go into stores, try on a million things, and buy nothing," she says.

Of course, I wonder if she's going to the right stores, or trying on the right cuts.

"It's hard to look in the mirror and not like what you see. I've tried to change. I've done Weight Watchers twice," she says. "But the hips are still here. Whenever I look at myself, my eyes go straight to my hips. I know I lack confidence and compensate by being self-deprecating. I grew up with all women. We beat ourselves up. It's what we do."

Beating yourself up is not a requirement for being a woman, although it is all too common. I wonder who's the particular "we" Sarah is referring to, though—the women she grew up with,

or women in general? Women do tend to beat themselves up endlessly. Unrealistic standards of perfection encourage us to be something impossible. That's bound to affect all of us to some degree.

I wish Sarah would give herself a P.A.S., aka a Positive Acceptance of Self. ✳ Every woman—and man—in the world has some issue with the way she or he looks, wishing that certain parts of their body were smaller, bigger, shorter, or longer. You're allowed to have those issues. But unless you can accept what you don't like about yourself, your style problem will only get worse. You'll try to hide in clothes, rather than "consciously camouflaging" the parts you don't like and highlighting what you love. Hiding and hating really suck the joy out of style, and put the victim in fashion. Above and beyond all that, Sarah needs reminding that she, as much as anyone, *deserves* to look and feel great. Lucky for me, Sarah was wearing clothes that fit her when she showed up. So part one was there, but the joy wasn't.

✳Positive Acceptance of Self: I love an acronym almost as much as a superlative. A P.A.S. is really like a pass. Like a hall pass to go hang out in the girls' bathroom during algebra (not that I'm encouraging that kind of behavior). Or, like in Monopoly, in which you get to pass Go and collect two hundred dollars (not that I'm giving you any money). In other words, it's a good thing: Allow your self-assessment to be based on hope, not on dissatisfaction. I'd like to thank David—the same awesome dude I mentioned in the introduction of this book and who turned me on to "Yes! . . . And?"—for this acronym. He's a fount of inspiration for me, as is his wife, Molly. They also throw a mean shabbos dinner, but I digress.

"When I do find clothes that fit, I feel joy," Sarah acknowledges. "I love clothes, but they don't love me. That's the sad part. It's a one-sided relationship."

Is there any aspect of shopping that isn't torture for Sarah?

"Weirdly, I have a normal shoe size. It's great that I can always find a shoe that fits," she says. "But I don't wear a lot of heels. Mainly flats. Very simple. I don't want to draw attention to my feet, because I have really fat ankles."

Crash. Burn. Bummer. Path to joy, thwarted. Even her footwear—which could be a universe of opportunity—doesn't bring her joy or make her feel sexy. And the truth is, her ankles aren't even close to being fat. It's generally true that no one sees you the way you see yourself, and that you are your own harshest critic. I've come across this mild form of body dysmorphia in a lot of other women I've worked with, including myself. What Sarah sees in the mirror does not reflect reality. And she believes what she sees to the exclusion of anyone else's opinion. That belief is reinforced by her difficulty finding clothes that work for her. She is not completely unjustified in being frustrated, only in beating herself up endlessly about it. (Actually, I had an interesting discussion with my friend Molly's sister, Tracy. She thinks—and she totally won me over—that we humans are wired to try to prove ourselves right. We look for proof of what we believe and feel justified in our beliefs when we find it. We never stop to think that our beliefs might be wrong.)

I wonder if she likes anything about her body.

"I have nice teeth," she concedes. "My dad's a dentist."

Well, I don't dress teeth. (But, to quote Dr. Seuss, "Teeth are always in style." And she does have nice ones.) I ask again about her body, but Sarah won't admit to admiring *any* part of herself below the neck. She can't turn away from what's "wrong" with her shape to assess the whole picture. When she starts trying stuff on, she can't even really see what she's wearing, because she's so preoccupied with every tiny detail below the waist. She obsesses about how her ankle looks against the narrow strap of a shoe instead of noticing or commenting on the bright purple top or a great pencil skirt. This is microfocusing. If she can't see what her body *could* look like, she can't *feel* how beautiful she is.

I Get It

While working with Sarah, I realize that we all receive the challenges in life we need. Sarah and I have some remarkable emotional similarities. My challenge is to come face-to-face with someone who may be just as defensive as me. Self-consciousness has affected my life, too, in both superficial and meaningful ways.

I also hate being photographed. I extremely dislike almost every photograph that's been taken of me. Publicity shots? Terrible. Magazine profiles and covers? Horrifying. I quake at some of the photos of me in advertisements. I'm fine in front of a TV or video camera, because in that context I can distract viewers with words, motions, sarcasm, and humor. Still photography, on the other hand, captures a two-dimensional split-second image in time. However much I try desperately to appear happy and relaxed, in the end I usually look tense and miserable. It doesn't matter if I'm heavier or thinner (remember, I'm a fluctuater) or having a good face day. Nine out of ten pictures of me make me recoil. But then I might see a random picture from five years ago and think, *I looked good! Why didn't I appreciate it then?* Like oodles of women, I have little sense of perspective.

Now, you might look at the cover of this book, and think, *Stacy looks confident there.* As I mentioned, I've gained weight in the past year. I am quick to blame it on global warming, planetary oscillations, and junk-food fairies who feed me in my sleep. Regardless of where they came from, the pounds arrived, and like rude dinner guests, they won't leave. I was trying not to bum out at the shoot for the cover, as I could easily have let those pounds render me incapable of standing in front of the camera. But I gave myself a daily dose of C^3 (Courage, Confidence, and a sense of positive Control) and powered through it. Choosing to wear a kickass Alexander McQueen dress helped a lot. My point (and I do have one): It's not that I'm not self-conscious. It's not even that I don't sometimes get paralyzed by it. But I, and Sarah, both have to try and overcome it.

In a deeper, more important, way, self-consciousness has often negatively affected my relationships, and even my overall happiness. I think it all goes back to the "something's wrong with me" message from childhood. The more defenseless, insecure, and vulnerable I felt, the stronger my defenses toward other people became. And I constructed some pretty big defenses. Fortunately for Sarah, she's only been feeling this level of self-consciousness for a few years. She may find it easier to pull herself out of that negative thinking, since I've got the jump on her by sixteen years.

Ever since I can remember I've had a talent for lashing out. As a child, anger provided me protection and ensured that people wouldn't hurt me. Fast-forward to being an adult: That same anger has pushed them away. It's led to burned bridges and has ended friendships that I realize only now could have been handled a lot differently by me, rather than defensively. Pretty sweet realization, really.

The other go-to defense mechanism Sarah and I share is self-deprecation. It's about beating the aggressor to the punch—as if other people are always going to be aggressive in the first place. That, in and of itself, is a big presupposition. I've expected others to treat me as badly as I beat myself up in my own head. Because I think the worst, I worry that they may think the worst, and I've made preemptive strikes without provocation. There are times when people do say the wrong thing but don't necessarily intend to wound with it. For the chronic self-deprecator, though, nothing people say—positive or negative—is heard through the right filter. Depending on the mood you're in, even "You're gorgeous!" can be taken the wrong way.

It's taken a while for me to understand that taking responsibility for my behavior requires me to take responsibility for my insecurity. I have to make choices that benefit me in the long run, and lashing

out isn't one of them. Neither is hating my body or assuming others do. But if I assume they do, no matter what they say, they're always going to seem like the enemy. While defense mechanisms can be elaborate security blankets, they don't allow for hearing something positive or appreciating genuinely helpful criticism, and that's ultimately as unhealthy as it is unproductive. To create intimacy, open communication, and a feeling of safety with other people, one has to take a less defensive position. I've learned that walls don't let anyone in, for good or ill.

Part of the reason for writing this book—and why I can even admit to having these thoughts—is that it took a long time for me to see that some of my negativity wasn't based in reality. I could talk about style as an agent of positive change for others while I allowed my own negative toxic-thinking loop to get in my own way. It's not that I was being hypocritical so much as that I simply wasn't seeing or taking my own advice. And we all know that's way harder to do than to dish it out to others. I have found that learning to acknowledge my discomfort (whether with my body, in certain social situations, or when faced with criticism) and trying to make it less toxic does change my thought process. The very act of noticing defensiveness can stop the negativity loop and keep it from spilling out onto others. (Neuroplasticity triumphs again.)

Circling back to Sarah's self-consciousness and her laser focus on the parts of her body she hates, I completely understand what she's feeling, and I suspect that she's got some serious defenses in place. It's easy to be your own worst critic, and to let your doubts and fears take over. It's harder to be your own impartial witness—but that is exactly what we need to be about our bodies. Otherwise, our anxieties will keep us from doing what we really want to accomplish in our lives. I don't want to minimize the fact that Sarah's body is harder to dress than some. But she can change how she *thinks* about it. Instead of saying, "It's impossible to find pants," she can reframe her attitude by saying, "It's difficult to find them." That's a big difference in mind-set. "Impossible" forces you to give up; "difficult" means you're in for a challenge. When you do achieve the style you want, you can begin to let go of the self-consciousness and self-deprecation.

Sarah's Start-over

THE SYMPTOM:

Blank-slate clothing due to frustration with fit

THE UNDERLYING CAUSES:

Self-consciousness, tunnel vision (she can only see what's "wrong," to the exclusion of all else)

THE PRESCRIPTION:

Systematic shopping: cross-department shopping and reality checks to dispel body distortion

Sarah's current self-consciousness makes self-knowledge impossible. She'll have to make a subtle but seismic shift in perspective, to assess and accept her actual proportions and thereby straighten out the funhouse mirror in her mind that's distorting them. She's tall (not a giant). Her hips are curvy (not gigantic). She has ankles (not cankles). Tall and curvy and disproportionate—top smaller, bottom larger—is the reality. We can work with that. The giantess she thinks she is? It's an unhealthy fantasy fed by insecurity and fueled by shopping frustration that has taken over Sarah's image of herself.

Because of her height, she *will* have a hard time finding pants that are long enough. Where style is concerned, she will have to pick her battles. It's not the end of the world to have only a few pairs of pants in her wardrobe. They might be plain, but

Ruching, seaming, pleating, stitching, and embellishment details on cotton-jersey shirts make them more interesting and expensive looking than a T-shirt. This is a great way to make a personal style statement without spending tons of money.

While I love when tall women embrace their height and wear heels, flats are functional (and necessary for Sarah's job), but they should just never, ever look like you are apologizing for your height—especially in the evening—so look for shoes that have cool eye-catching details and make a deliberate choice.

she can dress them up with great, brightly colored blouses, jewelry, and accessories. Or she can fully embrace skirts and dresses, which, despite her claim that she can't find *any*, are easier to fit than trousers. Because of her much smaller shoulders, her hips can appear wider—but creating a broader shoulder is possible with more voluminous tops, and stronger shoulder emphasis, like a shoulder pad.

Sarah might have to shop in three different departments to come up with a single outfit. For tops she can go with

If pants are hard, keep in mind that skirts are easier to fit on everyone. Well-tailored skirts are something to embrace, and while wearing them in the child-care field may be hard, Sarah should also be thinking about what she likes to dress in—what brings her joy—when she isn't working. Skirts could be beneficial to her future career trajectory. Plus, her hubby loves her in skirts and dresses.

mainstream sizing. For bottoms she may need plus size or missy. For keeping her look young and trendy she can wear fun accessories. It will take a lot of effort and time to go department to department and develop her personal style, but proactivity itself is a part of the solution. She'll be forced to spend a lot of time looking in the mirror and stepping in and out of clothes, thereby wearing down her aversion to fitting rooms, helping establish intimacy with her (real) body, and enabling her to see her real beauty. Sarah could also take a photo of herself every day—full length. By looking at it without any prejudice, she can learn from it, and also decide for herself what looks best on her.

Amass a jewelry and accessories collection to "trendify" wardrobe pieces that feel too matronly in either size or cut. At twenty-six, it's important for Sarah to stay modern. Even if she must cross-shop departments to find clothes that fit, accessories add a trend element to any outfit.

Why This Works

I wanted to use color and print to emphasize Sarah's upper half.

- **THE CARDIGAN:** The first thing we tried on Sarah is something beautiful, bold, and bright, like her. The colors work well with her skin tone and bring out her eye color. A cardigan and, even further, a cardigan with a floral print could age Sarah were it not for the modernity of this particular print and color palette. The abstract floral, almost watercolorlike print makes this appropriate for someone in her twenties. This sweater also has a slight shoulder pad to help broaden Sarah's top half.

- **THE SHIRT:** This striped shirt has an awesome figure-flattering detail: the tied knot sits slightly higher than Sarah's natural waistline, which draws the eye upward and highlights the smallest part of her torso. The solid white collar also keeps the focus toward her face. Mixing prints can be tricky, but there are a few rules of thumb: Stay in the same color palette and allow one to be the bolder focus. Here the traditional stripe of the shirt doesn't compete with the bold print of the cardigan—it just makes the combo look more interesting and inventive.

- **THE JEAN:** A dark-wash straight-leg jean is a wardrobe must-have. It acts as a blank slate on which you can create any style. These were the first pair of jeans she tried on, and—shocking!—they were long enough.

- **THE SHOES:** In the end, I did go with a flat for Sarah because they are the most practical for her life in child care right now. But the pointy toe lengthens her leg regardless of any heel absence. I encouraged Sarah to buy some heels and to embrace her inner glamazon.

- **THE JEWELRY:** While the earrings are hanging, they don't crowd Sarah's face. Be sure to check that the length of a hanging earring doesn't crowd your neck when you're wearing a collared shirt. I love this flower bracelet. It echoes the print of the sweater and just adds some whimsy to the whole outfit!

- **THE HAIR:** I am in love with this cut on Sarah. The bangs frame her face beautifully and the cut suits her age and lifestyle: young, not overdone, but pro-actively chic.

Yes!............................And?

Accept the unvarnished truth and build your style strategy from there.

"I'm self-conscious about my height, hips, legs, and ankles."

Great! So you know that about yourself. Be glad you have the awareness, but then look again at yourself—this time with a practical eye instead of a critical one. You don't help yourself by being self-conscious. But, with awareness and acceptance, you can figure out the steps to take to deal with your body issues through style. You can hate these body parts, work against them, deny them, or you can accept the reality of your shape and fit them—no matter how much work it takes to do it.

"I try on pair after pair of pants, but nothing fits."

A gross exaggeration that also does you no favors. If you go to a store and the pants are too tight, go up a size and take in the waist. If they're too short, try talls or letting out the seam allowance. Take control over your clothes. Don't just accept them as is. Tailoring is a powerful tool in and of itself. Manipulate and tame what you wear into submission. Be your own clothes whisperer. If a particular brand doesn't carry your size or inseam length, then don't go to that store again *for pants*. Also, accept that your choices with pants aren't going to be as extensive as what you can find in skirts, dresses, tops, shoes, jackets, and accessories. Find those few pairs of basic pants that fit, and make your style statement with the other pieces. *FYI: The two pairs of pants I tried on Sarah and the jeans she came in wearing both fit and were the right size. One pair I tried on her was even long enough to wear heels.*

"I can't . . . I never . . . I don't . . ."

Yes, you can, and often, and should. Whatever you think you can't do, you must do. It's true for conquering any fear, including the fear of showing your arms, or wearing heels, or putting on a form-fitting dress. By saying no you make things impossible for yourself. That's not giving yourself a P.A.S. The idea is to expand your ideas about style, not to cut them off at the knee. (No pun intended.) Next time you think, *No . . . never . . . don't . . .*, stop the negative thought loop, rewind it, and say, *How can I try this? What is my strategy? How can I be kind to myself?* And keep shopping until you do find your style solutions. You *DESERVE* this.

DON'T FEAR THE MIRROR

A solid foundation in personal style is built in the nude. Practically, you have to understand your canvas, your body, before you can use style as a tool for good and not evil. The only way is to look at yourself—*really* look. Do not flinch. Just look.

Nobody (and no body) is perfect. Don't approach the mirror and hope, each time, that you'll look like someone else. You're going to be disappointed if you do. As a body-image strategy, it's a sure loser. So is ignoring the areas you dislike to make them disappear. As an alternative to delusion and self-torture, how about simple honesty? Take a realistic appraisal. Go ahead and feel disgusted, embarrassed, cranky, and bitter about the parts you hate. Keep it up for as long as you need to, until you're able to look dispassionately at your body. When you can view yourself objectively, you can begin to strategize toward the way you wish to look with the raw material that has been given to you. Notice, don't judge. Noticing is just seeing what's there. Our judgment of it is what blinds us. The thick waist, big hips, small shoulders, anything, is not a flaw. It just is.

No matter how much you subjectively love or hate your shape, it's still the same body you're going to wake up with each morning. Stop exhausting yourself hoping, wishing, praying to be someone different, and take pleasure in knowing that you are who you are, in all your fabulous uniqueness. (Snowflake alert!) Go about the business of working with that real body to create a style you love and can love your shape in.

"Inaction breeds doubt and fear. Action breeds confidence and courage. If you want to conquer fear, do not sit and think about it. Go out and get busy."

—DALE CARNEGIE

TRACY

Dear Stacy:

I am a 33-year-old book sales rep in Missouri. I live with my boyfriend of eight
years and our dog Rudy. For fun and to stay in shape, I ballroom dance. I love
to bake and create cakes—love to eat them, too. My dream is to one day own
my own bakery.

I watch *What Not to Wear* every week. I've tried to learn from you how
to dress well and find my personal style. But every day, when I get dressed,
I always feel like something is missing. My clothes are uninspired. Part of
the problem is my job. I sell textbooks and software to colleges. I do a lot of
running around, and heavy lifting. Can't do that in heels and a pencil skirt. I
wind up wearing black pants and sweaters.

I need some sparkle, Stacy! I have been wearing the same few outfits for the
last three years. How boring!

Thank you for considering me!!
Tracy

It was Tracy's picture, and not her letter, that initially caught my attention. She was lovely, with gorgeous skin, and I love red hair! Plus, she wants to open a bakery, and I have never met a baked good I didn't like. But it wasn't evident to me what her style issue really was. She said she needed a tweak, and I was curious to see if that's all she needed.

When we meet at the studio, I see that the photo doesn't do her justice. She's totes adorbs. We get along right from the start. She's open with me, and laughs easily. She's a people person, for sure (sales rep). When she talks to me about hobbies she loves (baking and ballroom dancing), she just beams. Switch the conversation to style and it's as if the light goes out in her.

"'Boring' is the main word for my style," she says. "I try to wear clothes that are functional and won't get in the way. I never wear dresses or skirts. Always pants. Sometimes I have to run from one side of a college campus to the other in ten minutes, carting a huge suitcase and a laptop. I need speed, and comfort.

"Where I live, we don't have such great shopping. I go to midprice-range designer stores. I try to keep up with trends. I might wind up getting my entire wardrobe at one store, and it looks a lot like the same wardrobe I got there the year before," she explains. "My style is predictable, too. Uninspired. I wear the same thing every day to work: flats, pants, a sweater, a coat, and that's it. It's functional, but not exciting. Accessory-wise, I'm not so good with that, either. I buy belts, but I don't use them. I bought some wedge booties, but I never wear them. I have a degree in graphic design, and I even make jewelry. But I don't wear it, any of it. I want to make a change, but I don't know how."

She buys belts and shoes but doesn't wear them. She makes jewelry but it sits in the drawer. She's got a degree in graphic design, and she can't put a visually interesting outfit together? Clearly, she's an artistic person. She has an eye. The fact that Tracy doesn't apply her knowledge of color and pattern to how she dresses is a major disconnect. My suspicion is that she doesn't trust her own instinct or use her artistic sensibility. But why not?

This morning, she's wearing jeans and a black sweater, her self-described uninspired clothes. I'd just call them "a snore fest." Has she always been a drab dresser?

"When I was little I'd put on the biggest, poofiest dress and twirl. I loved dresses and skirts then. I loved to twirl. I'd see a dress in a bright color and think, *That looks fun! I'm going to wear it.*

"It's been a really long time since I opened my closet and felt happy and excited about my options," she admits. "Nowadays, I only wear a dress if I have a special occasion. If I went to the supermarket in a dress, I'd feel self-conscious, like people were looking at me, thinking, *Why is she all dressed up?* They'd judge me for trying to show off or draw attention to myself. I don't know if it's a bad thing to try to get attention based on your clothes. I just don't want anyone looking at me when I'm shopping. I mean, I'm just there to run in and out. It might feel weird to go to the grocery store in a skirt for a loaf of bread. I don't want to be judged." *

Lost the urge to twirl? That's terrible. And what is she talking about, not wanting to wear a dress to the market so no one will watch her buy bread?

She puts her hands up, a gesture of frustration. "I'm intimidated by fashion,

*__News flash:__ You will be judged, whether you want to be or not. According to studies, it takes three seconds for people to form an opinion based on someone's looks. In the length of a sneeze, a stranger will classify you in his mind without having spoken to you or knowing a single concrete thing about you. Style is *visual currency.* Your appearance has value to yourself and others, be they friends or strangers. You can put on a sweatshirt and hope that it'll render you invisible. But that's willful blindness to the truth. You won't be invisible, even if you try to be (unless you have a magic cape). Take comfort in the fact that most people are not half as harsh or observant as you might fear. Most of the time they're so preoccupied with themselves, they don't notice you anyway. You are probably a far harsher critic than anyone walking behind you on the street. Although you might suspect someone's staring at your butt and thinking it looks fat, or lumpy, or that it wriggles like two cats fighting in a bag, he or she's probably not. It's insecurity blown out of proportion. If you took a poll of one hundred people and asked, "Does my ass look fat?" ninety-four of them would say, "Uh, who are you?"

maybe because I don't understand how to make it work for me," she says. "I don't want to be frilly, tacky, or gaudy. Ideally, I'd have functional clothes that are fun."

Sounds to me like she's having confusion about situational appropriateness—there are some dresses that you can wear to buy bread that no one would describe as gaudy or tacky, and some dresses you can reserve for twirling. At this point, anything other than utilitarian black pants and a sweater would be an improvement for Tracy. But more than expanding the utility of her wardrobe, it seems like she needs to reconnect to the joy of dressing. Her anxiety that people might think she's calling undue attention to herself with style has robbed it of fun.

"I felt judged a lot in high school and college. I had my own sense of style, wore what was fun, and didn't think much about it. People told me I looked crazy," she says. "I got that *label*. Then I switched to jeans and sweatshirts, thinking, *Well, this is what everyone else has on. I can't go wrong there*."

Well, she has now.

Tracy is thirty-three. College ended twelve years ago. Did she go straight from jeans and sweats to boring pants and black sweaters?

"I tried to dress better right after college," she says. "But then, about five years ago, I started my current job selling textbooks. I have meetings with professors every day and need to look kind of professional. A lot of the time I never even take off my coat."

What I'm hearing is that Tracy willfully lets herself blend in and has stopped trusting her own instincts. Her current job seems to dictate what Tracy will wear, and her style is symbolic of where she is in her career right now. They're both placeholders, or what she's doing before she pursues her real dreams. But more than that, her job has given her an excuse to dress "safely." The pants and sweater are her version of a uniform. She needs to be comfortable and look a certain way for work, which are legitimate concerns, no matter what your job is. But even for running around to meetings with conservative professors, she can still have fun as well as function, and achieve the style upgrade she says she desperately wants. Her future ought to include cupcakes and color.

Color first.

"I'd like to stand out more, and not just blend in. But I don't have the knowledge of how to do it," she admits. "I'm scared about screwing up and dressing in a way that's *too* stylish."

This is a *total* disconnect with the woman whom I see sitting before me. We're a long way from too stylish. But really, I want to know who she thinks she is *not* to stand out. With all that glorious hair, she can't help but draw attention.

"I'm self-conscious of what I put on. I don't want someone to think I look trashy," she continues.

Gaudy, trashy, frilly? What was said to her in high school or college? I wonder to myself where this vocabulary of words comes from. The truth is, when I ask her about her taste, it runs toward the classic. She couldn't look trashy if she tried. And, FYI, sparkle isn't trashy—it's *sparkly.* Tracy seems to think anything other than trousers and a black crewneck sweater is somehow daring, and an invitation for criticism. Talk about too many excuses.

Does she use bright-colored frosting on her cupcakes?

"Of course!"

What about her dream of opening a bakery someday?

"I don't know how to get from textbooks to cupcakes," she says. "I haven't done anything to open a bakery because I don't know how. I'm a little afraid to go for it."

This is the second time I've heard her say "I don't know how." But not knowing how to get started is not an excuse for not doing it. Sometimes, attacking a smaller goal leads to achieving bigger ones. In other words, first a colorful outfit. Then, who knows?

✳Fear-based dressing is the most common thing on the planet. It's style nitrogen. Tracy would rather hide in her closet than put on an outfit that stands out. Her fear comes from having been ridiculed in the past for her so-called crazy style. So she's gone full speed in the opposite direction, into the safe and invisible. Her instincts, deeply buried, are telling her she needs more. Fear mixed with aspiration is the recipe for baking a conflict cupcake.

What's the worst thing that someone could say about an outfit of hers?

"'Who do you think you are?'"

Is that really so bad? There's absolutely nothing Tracy or any of us can do about the private thoughts and reactions of other people. We can't control them. We can only concern ourselves with our own thoughts and feelings. Obviously, we all want positive reinforcement from the outside world. And yes, people judge based on appearance. So we can try to hide forever in fear—or allow ourselves to shine. Let others benefit from the joy we share with them and ignore the ones who aren't up for sharing.✳

How to start shining? As always, start with *you.* I ask: "What do you love about yourself?"

"I like my arms, especially from the elbow down," Tracy offers. "I like my hair.

And my calves. I'm good from the knees down. And my thighs are okay. I have a pair of skinny jeans," she says.

And does she wear them?

"No."

I'm starting to see a pattern here: Tracy has belts, wedge booties, jewelry, and skinny jeans. If she just looked in her closet, she could have a stronger style.

Next I ask, "What do you not like about yourself?"

"I hate my big hips," Tracy says. "And I don't like my midsection. I had surgery when I was six that left scars on my back and side. I feel kind of lopsided because of it. My left side comes in farther than my right. Everyone says they can't see it. They don't look at me and say, 'You're deformed.' I see the difference when I wear clingy tops. I usually throw a big blazer or sweater over it. It's an issue, but I don't think it's major."

Well, if it's not major, don't hide in oversize blazers or sweaters.

Next: "What makes you happy to wear?"

"My favorite color is yellow," she says. "Bright yellow. And I like red. You can't have a bad day in a bright red skirt."

True. Do you wear one?

"No."

Quel surprise.

I Get It

Like Tracy, I've experienced the feeling that the minute you walk into a room, people turn to look at you. Some steal peeks out of the corner of their eyes. Some stare right at you. You can practically see their thoughts like a neon sign: *Who does she think she is?*

I've heard that refrain for the last ten years, ever since I debuted on television in 2002. It's one that's played in my own head and asked outright by anonymous commenters, media critics, and unfriendly strangers. Just as you're not necessarily paranoid if people really are out to get you, it's not a narcissistic delusion to think people are staring at you and giving you the once-over five times if they tweet about it later that day. Or if they post a status update on your Facebook wall that says, "Your nose is huge. You should get that fixed. Why haven't you?" Or if they analyze your weight ups and downs as obsessively as the stock market. Or if they blog about how "kind of hippy" and "small on top" you are.

(For the record, I would never get a nose job. I was born with my nose. I like it. It makes sense as the centerpiece of my face. I wouldn't be me with a cookie-cutter ski-slope nose. For the same reason, I don't dye my gray streak. I like how it looks and consider it my trademark—not as in ™; I haven't registered Gray Streak with the Trademark Office. Like my nose, it's part of the combination of features that makes me who I am.)

Even the bravest among us (not me) would be shaken by this level of scrutiny. I do feel anxious about being judged, in the public square and in private rooms, as unfashionable and unattractive. If I hit the street without makeup or didn't carefully plan my outfit to the smallest detail, there's always the worry that someone will say or think, "OMG, in real life, Stacy London is a hideous slob. Who the hell is she to tell other people . . . ? Where does she get off . . . ? She thinks she's so . . ." etc.

All this comes with the territory. I've spent twenty-two years styling other people. All you need are 10,000 hours to be an expert. I'd say I'm qualified. But my being on camera instead of behind it now opens the door wide for anyone with an opinion on fashion or style—or noses and hips, for that matter—to knock me. We live in a time when, literally, everyone is a critic. The minute you open your mouth anywhere in the media, you're

fair game to be judged. The comments sometimes hurt my feelings. But if I let the harsh judgments of others stop me, I might as well never leave my apartment. I have strong convictions, and that's one of the reasons people listen to me. If I just complimented everyone, then my advice wouldn't help anyone.

We all have to learn to shrug off criticism (the destructive, mean kind). If you feel and have the knowledge that what you're doing is right for you, then screw anyone who says otherwise. That's also true of style. I understand Tracy's fear of judgment about the theoretical person who would react negatively to one of her outfits. But you're the only one living your life, wearing your clothes, and walking in your shoes. Primarily, you've just got to please yourself. If anyone does break the fourth wall of polite society and says to your face, "Who do you think you are?" channel your inner Elizabeth Taylor. There's a great scene in *Butterfield 8*, the role for which Elizabeth Taylor got her first Oscar: A lurching drunk at a bar propositions La Liz in an aggressive, hostile way. She basically tells him to piss off. In anger, he asks, "Who do you think you are?"

She snaps, "I'm *me*!"

Ha!

Tracy's Start-over

THE SYMPTOM:

A style-rut drab uniform of pants and a black sweater

THE UNDERLYING CAUSE:

Fear, in a few manifestations: (1) of being judged, (2) of fashion, (3) of standing out, (4) of her own instincts

THE PRESCRIPTION:

Dress-Out-Loud style replaces Hide-in-Plain-Sight invisibility

Everything about Tracy—her smile, voice, ballroom dancing, baking, jewelry making—conveys that she's an exuberant, alive woman. When I first saw her photo, I thought, *She's so cute. She just needs a tweak.* But after meeting her, and seeing the disconnect between her and her style, I realized that she needs more than fine-tuning.

Only Tracy knows what it means personally to feel joy about what she's wearing. She did earlier in her life, and she can easily reconnect with the way she used to feel.

Fear is stopping her. It's made her numb to the emotional experience of dressing for joy. She's lost touch with the instincts that drew her to twirltastic dresses. It takes effort to switch off fear and see yourself in a new way. I can visualize Tracy in a bright, sparkly outfit, standing behind the counter of her own bakery, a display case filled with beautiful cupcakes. My question is: Can she see it?

My goal isn't to impose my own vision for her on her; I'm just going with what she says she wants for herself: To get out of her rut and dress with as much yumminess as she would frost a cupcake, Tracy has to take action to overcome her fear. She's right in her belief that style does take knowledge and work. But anyone can do it.

A joy injection is achieved by dressing out loud. Joy isn't a whimper in the corner. It's living and dressing with your full throat. We all deserve to be seen and heard, to get positive attention and respect, and to know we're worthy of it. If you truly feel that way about yourself, and/ or you want to use style to get you there, pump up the volume in your outfits. And by volume, I don't mean mass or bulk. I mean see them, and hear them, and make them sing! Just remember: There is such a thing as going overboard. You do have to give a slight nod to convention. I wouldn't tell someone who loves rainbows to wear them head to toe or someone who loves unicorns to wear a horn hat and hoof

Color, pattern, and shine are the hallmarks of joy-based dressing. When you are afraid of these things, start small, by adding them to your wardrobe with accessories such as scarves, bags, belts, and jewelry.

Print blouses are another easy and flattering way to add patterns to your wardrobe without going overboard. Pair them with solid colors, neutrals, or denim to keep the outfit grounded. Prints also allow you to convey your personality. Which prints you're attracted to and wear communicates a lot about your personal taste. Just as your general guide: florals = feminine; geometrics = strong and authoritative; abstracts = modern and artistic.

Denim is a great wardrobe chameleon. You can wear it to work or dress it up for evenings or dress down with it on weekends. Think of it as a blank canvas to test out trends that might be too risky head to toe. No one in the world—of any size or age—can't rock a good trouser jean. As Nylon magazine once printed, "If you can't tell if your jeans look good in 30 seconds, you need a better pair."

clogs. I like a 75-25 split: 75 percent of your style choices should be about making you happy; 25 percent can be about what you're transmitting to others and making a good impression to help you get what you want out of life.

If others don't appreciate it, that's their problem. Yes, people can be harsh critics. Mean people suck. But how you're seen by casual observers and friends, bosses, neighbors, or the cashier at the supermarket is not as important as how you judge yourself. When Tracy was younger, some idiot called her "crazy," and she relinquished 100 percent of her style to what others were saying. In high school, it was dangerous to be different. As an adult in a crowded world? Standing out may be just the thing you need in order to succeed.

Do not let what happened to you in high school rule your life now.

One last thought: Tracy doesn't always have to know why something works, or when, or how. Joy is about just going for it. It's the exuberance of spontaneity and letting instinct guide you. It requires a leap of faith that, if you mull about it forever, might not happen. As a student of philosophy, I don't often say this, but in some cases, thinking is overrated. Sometimes just *doing* is more important.

To reiterate: Jackets must *close across the chest. That's part of their job. If they don't close, they don't fit. Go up a size. If the jacket is then too big in the shoulder, it can be altered and reset. This is an expensive alteration (so consider other jackets as options first) but possible and necessary especially if you have narrow shoulders and carry your weight in your chest or midsection.*

Why This Works

In one outfit, Tracy gets everything that was missing in her wardrobe.

• **THE SKIRT:** She said it: "You can't have a bad day in a bright red skirt"—or a tangerine-red one, either. It's feminine. A straight skirt frames the lower half of her well-proportioned body and highlights her curves.

• **THE BLOUSE:** The tie front is inherently feminine without being tacky, gaudy, or too frilly. The black-and-white print is subtle but visible enough to add some visual interest to the outfit based in solid colors.

• **THE CARDIGAN:** There are few people in the world who can't wear fuchsia. It's one of those great colors that's flattering on everyone. This particular fuchsia is of the same saturation value as the red skirt. So while both colors are bright, they're equally bright, which balances the entire proportion of the outfit. Look for thin knits to wear over blouses, so that they don't add bulk and are figure flattering. The fit of this sweater shows that she's got a great rack without pulling anywhere.

• **THE BELT:** Always great to cinch a waist but more importantly for Tracy, a belt in a great color is a little "somethin'"—somethin' she can always throw on to punch up neutral basics.

• **THE BAG:** Tracy loves yellow. Because it can be a hard color to wear, it's always easier to incorporate it (and any other favorite challenging colors) into your wardrobe with a purse or a shoe.

• **THE SHOES:** High, shiny neutral, to die for. Who doesn't feel happier in a glorious heel? Okay, okay, not for eighteen hours a day, but still. A wedge or pointy-toe flat are other options for longer day wear.

Pulled apart, each piece works with the life she has now. Tracy might never wear this exact outfit for work, but she can put the sweater and blouse with jeans or neutral-colored trousers. The skirt, with a sparkly top, would be great at a wedding or on a date with her boyfriend.

There are a million reasons for Tracy to have each of these pieces in her wardrobe, not the least of which is, they make her happy. Look at that face! The proof is in the *punim*.*

---

*Punim: Yiddish for "face." And if you don't know that already, shande on you.

Yes!.................And?

Accept the unvarnished truth and build your style strategy from there.

"I want to dress better, but I don't know how."

Then learn! What does "I don't know how" signify? It means "I'm willing to let fear rule my life." You can't express a desire and then stand still and not *do* something about it. (I know. I have to learn how to drive...) You're not allowed to let "I don't know how" put your life and style on pause. If you want color and sparkle in your wardrobe, if you miss wearing sparkly dresses and skirts, GET IN 'EM. Go to the store, today, and at least start trying stuff on.

"I used to wear bright colors, and people called me crazy."

Where are those people now? Do you care? Does it matter in your life what some idiot said fifteen years ago? Your happiness with what you're wearing carries more weight than the comments of kids whose names you probably can't even remember. It bears repeating: Do not let what happened to you in the past rule your life now.

"I'm afraid someone might say something if I wore a red dress to the grocery store."

Well, (1) Who cares what they say? And (2) You know what they'd say if you wore jeans and a baggy black shirt? Nothing. (Well, not "nothing"; see chart, next page.) And you'll feel nothing by wearing them. So zero people in this equation have any emotional reaction at all. Take the risk and wear bright clothes that bring you joy. As far as other people go, it's always 50-50 how they'll react anyway. Some will like it, some might not. But instead of zero emotional reaction, you get 100 percent personal satisfaction. You have to get past second-guessing what other people might think and just wear what makes you happy. Just do what makes you happy, period.

TRANSMISSION VS. TRANSLATION

Sometimes when we dress out of fear, we wind up transmitting exactly what we don't want to say about ourselves. In our effort to hide or appear as if we don't care about our style, we end up transmitting incorrect assumptions, an even stronger reason to dress with conviction, intention, and joy!

OVERSIZE CLOTHES
Transmission:
I'm comfortable.

Translation:
I'm hiding.

PLAIN UTILITARIAN CLOTHES
Transmission:
I'm above fashion.

Translation:
I'm afraid of fashion.

ALL BLACK AND DARK CLOTHES
Transmission:
Don't mess with me.

Translation:
Don't look at me.

TOO-TIGHT CLOTHES
Transmission:
I'm desirable.

Translation:
I'm desperate.

SUPER-QUIRKY CLOTHES
Transmission:
I'm a free spirit.

Translation:
I'm an outpatient.

SLOPPY OR STAINED CLOTHES
Transmission:
I shrug.

Translation:
I smell.

"I think, therefore I'm single."

—LIZZ WINSTEAD

ANNIE

Dear Stacy:

My name is Annie. I'm 48, but I'm always told I look younger. I live in a small Indiana town, but I would like to feel like I live in the Big Apple! My style: For work in a medical lab, I like to be always "meeting ready," just in case I need to see a client unexpectedly. I wear dresses and heels but stick to the safe zone of black. I've got two grown kids. My twenty-year-old daughter likes to help me when I dress casually, but I personally have not found my casual-style comfort zone. I don't want to dress old but don't want to dress like I am trying to look young.

Five years ago, I divorced after a 25-year marriage. He initiated, and I did not see it coming. I'm positive that everything happens for a reason, though. I put my social life on hold until my kids were both in college. I am just now thinking of dating, which I haven't done since I was 19. It's a whole new world out there. So here I am basically entering a new phase/next phase of my life. I'm excited to begin again, but I need to find a confident put-together version of me. I recently lost twenty-eight pounds by doing yoga, Zumba, kickboxing and training for my first 5K. I finished and DID NOT DIE! I'm at a good weight now. I still have curves and like it.

Please consider me to have my style reinvented for my new phase of life!!!

Best Regards,
Annie

My first reaction to Annie is that her body is totally fierce. (She does Zumba, just like Tania. Apparently, it's the new Pilates.) I'm not as impressed by her jeans. They're too young for her, with heavy top-stitching and lots of bleaching. Dressing like a college kid when you're the mom of a coed can make you look older than you really are. (Yep, pinch, ouch.)

When we sit down on the couch, she's bursting to tell her story, and I'm eager to hear it. With her high energy, Annie is engaging and so likable. Her eyes are the awesomesauciest dark blue.

"I married my high school sweetheart at nineteen," she says. "Not every marriage is perfect, but I thought ours was solid. On New Year's Eve several years ago he just said, 'I don't love you anymore. I want a divorce.' The divorce was official five years ago—exactly. Today is the anniversary."

Uh, congratulations?

"We tried to keep it peaceful for the kids—my son was twelve and my daughter was fifteen at the time of the split," she says. "My ex still lives less than a mile from me. We see each other every day. The kids have a good relationship with him."

Impressive. Divorce without drama is hard and admirable. Annie is obviously an upbeat person. And yet, her style—a black shirt, her too-young jeans—doesn't reflect her upbeat energy. She looks like a bit of a downer, to be honest. Although that could just be me. . . . She's the ninth woman I've seen in a black top and jeans. (It's tough to be last.)

"I put my life on hold until the kids were more or less out of the house," she says. "My daughter, now twenty, is a junior in college, and my son, seventeen, starts in the fall. I'm ready to begin my next phase and start dating. But I need to find me first. I've been someone's wife or someone's mother since I was nineteen. I have to figure out who I am.

"My whole world has changed. New house. New friends. Some of my old friends stood by me. But others . . . didn't," Annie says. "When I stopped being part of a couple, they stopped inviting me. They don't let singles in. It's weird. I've felt a bit lost. Everything about my old life has changed, save for the kids. My wardrobe should change, too." ✳

Divorce is one of those life situations that changes everything. And a change in style to match a new stage of life, and persona, can help ease that transition. Because, let's face it: Change is freaking hard. Dating for the first time in almost thirty years? That's a lot of downtime and is going to require some super-*chutzpah*.

"Chutzpah": Yiddish for "guts."

"Maybe I could have started dating sooner," Annie acknowledges. "My husband did right away, but I think that shook up the kids. I might have used them as an excuse to hide from dating for a while—kids are good for that. But now I don't have them for an excuse anymore," she says. "They want me to focus on myself. My daughter wants me to date. Even they know I shut down my social life out of fear. I've detoured it long enough. I've got to get to where I feel comfortable with myself before I begin. That's why I'm here."

Annie takes a long, deep breath. "You know those bracelets that say 'What Would Jesus Do?' Well, one of my best friends of twenty years, Sheri, and I always said, 'What would Stacy London do?' when we shopped. Then Sheri got sick with melanoma. The doctors gave her three months, but she lived for two years. Not once in all that time did she complain or

✳ **Part of the famous** Henry David Thoreau quote comes to mind, "Beware of all enterprises that require new clothes." That's *bullshit*. I think Thoreau was spot-on about appreciating nature, etc., but he was dead wrong about clothes. Style, when it's successful, is a visual representation of your situation and attitude. Your personality and circumstances change dramatically over time, so your style should, too. If you want to signal an emotional turn, you can change your style. So be happy about enterprises that require new clothes—no bewaring necessary. Sorry, Henry. Don't take it personally. Love your work.

get depressed. For most of her illness, she didn't even look sick. Sheri stayed positive and felt pretty good until right before the end. A few months before she died, she told me, 'Live. Just *live*. Don't be afraid of anything.' When she said that, I was on the fence about sending in a letter to be part of this book, but her words really hit me. I want to *live*, to date again, even though I'm terrified. She convinced me to push past my fears, and I sent in my letter to you.

"She died a few weeks ago," Annie says quietly. "I was walking back to my car after the funeral service, very upset, and that's when I got the e-mail from you, inviting me to be a part of this book. I burst into tears. I really believe the positive energy we put out into the world comes back. I feel like I honor Sheri's memory by being active and trying to take risks. I ran my first 5-K recently, and I have lost a ton of weight. I'm ready to begin. But I don't know how to dress for it."

It takes me a minute to respond to this story. It feels so sad, but at the same time, I can't help but think: *Sheri, if you're up there? I'm going to do my best for Annie.*

"My big question for you is, what's age appropriate for dating at forty-eight?" Annie asks. "I see women my age dressing in clothes too tight, too short, too low. They come off like cheap, desperate sluts, with the girls hanging out. I definitely don't want to come off like that!"

As if I would *ever* let Annie come off as cheap or desperate! She does raise a critical point, though: How *does* a single woman in her forties (sound like anyone else we know?) dress for dating in a way that'll make her feel empowered, sexy, and confident? It can be a toughie.

"My current style is wearing a lot of black. Black is how I fly under the radar. Color is 'want to be seen,'" Annie says. "If I'm between sizes, I go bigger to hide my body. My clothes still reflect some

fear. My daughter says, 'Don't hide, Mom.' She's right. I play it safe. But I definitely don't want to call too much attention to myself and freak out my dates."

And since when do dates "freak out" if a girl wears color? Who'd want to date him anyway?

Where's the happy medium? Not wanting to look like a desperate slut doesn't mean hiding in oversize black clothes, either. Everyone is multidimensional. There are the days you may need to wear black (but it should fit) and feel hidden from the world, and there are days you wear bright purple and come out swinging.

"No matter what, I always wear makeup when I leave the house," she continues. *

"You might meet Prince Charming or your worst enemy at Walmart," she says. "More likely, though, I'll run into a neighbor. I live in a small town, and it's like a soap opera. I know too much about everyone.

I have a strategy to meet someone new. I should go to the places where I'll find the kind of man I want. If I want a generous man, I should go to a charity event. If I want an athletic man, I'll go hiking and camping. If I want a businessman, I'll volunteer at the chamber of commerce. This is why I don't go to bars to meet men."

So now I've got Annie's man-hunting strategy. What are *her* interests? If she did what she enjoyed, might not a man turn up

> **✳ Why is it that** women think it's okay if they wear makeup and do their nails and hair to go out of the house but then wear sweats or the denim equivalent? If they have time to put on a five-minute face, they can take four minutes and throw on a decent outfit, too.

looking for her? (One thing to reconsider: In her search for a generous, athletic businessman, should she be asking the question, Does this kind of man drink? So I wouldn't rule out bars altogether. Just my two cents.)✳

"I need to sort that out," she says. "When I was married I went places and dressed to please my husband. Now I have the idea that I need to be myself but dress to please my potential dates. What

I really need is to build up my courage and confidence to date again at all. The prospect is frightening. For better or for worse, I was with the same man for nearly thirty years. I was really comfortable with him. He saw me first thing in the morning, and last thing at night. It's daunting to try to find that comfort zone again with a new person. When he does come into my life, I want to be ready."

All right, Annie. Ready, set, date.

I Get It

I had my first "date date" (as in, not parentally supervised) at age thirteen. Twenty-nine years later, at forty-two, I'm a never-married, childless single woman. That is the hardest sentence I've written thus far in this book. I can talk about having had severe psoriasis and about the physical and psychological scars I carry around (neat little accessories) as a result. I can describe the internalizing

of bad intel from my childhood that made me feel like I was an alien. I'm upfront about my eating disorders, going from 90 to 180 pounds in a year, and all the fluctuations since. I can recount the humiliation of getting fired and being broke, my hermit tendencies. I've processed them all.

(And now so have you, my lucky little readers. Still with me?)

What can I say. I wear my heart on my sleeve . . . but at least it's a chic sleeve . . .

Annie's been married and has kids. She's from a small town in Indiana, and I live in New York City. Our lives are different, but we inhabit a similar landscape. Sometimes it seems as if there's only a barely perceptible stigma about being single. Lots of people go the movies alone, go to bars, and join couples on nights out. And then there are times when that barely perceptible stigma is like having a huge *S* stamped on your forehead. It goes in shifts. Friends don't ask about it. Then it's a constant barrage of people asking, "Why are you single?" "Do you date?" "Who are you seeing?" Wendy Williams has had me on her TV show a few times, and once she said, "You're just like Bethenny Frankel. Except she's married and has a baby, and you're single." *OUCH.* Wendy probably had no idea how sensitive I am about the subject (she might now, however), although anyone might feel a twinge of embarrassment over having her romantic ineptitude trumpeted on national TV. Yay, me.

I'm used to putting myself forward. It's part of my job. The demands of being out there in a romantic context, though, amp up the anxiety. You're trying to find the one person in the world who will look at you as the most important person in the world. How does that *ever* happen? It's like finding a particular grain of sand on the beach. A special needle in a haystack of

needles mixed with various grains in a silo (you get my point). What starts out as a near impossibility gets even harder as the years go by. When you're young, you're not as self-aware. You might be insecure, but you have some flexibility, some evolution still to come. Your quirks, habits, and needs aren't as dug in. When you're older, you're not as apt to change for someone else. I'm pretty rigid about my personal standards and habits, actually.

Awesomesauce advertisement for dating me, huh?

Maybe I'm addicted to being single. As upsetting as it seems in theory, I'm comfortable with it day-to-day. It's like an old sweatshirt for me (not that I wear old sweatshirts; okay, maybe to sleep . . . when I have a cold). Single is safe. At times I do wonder, though, if I am, actually, genuinely happy being on my own, or have I just convinced myself to think that way because I've given up hope? No one wants to be lonely. I don't know if I am. I do know that if I'm going to change my life to be with someone else, he'll have to be very, very . . . *something.*

I always thought I'd marry or at least wind up with a lifetime partner. In hindsight, though, I can see that this part of life has never come easy. I didn't fall in love until I was twenty-five. Before then I dated a little but never had a "real" boyfriend. All of my relationships, the ones that lingered (some have been on-again, off-again for years), were problematic almost from the start. It's not that I'm blaming the guys I dated. I made my choices.

In my early thirties I was dating a man who told me at the very beginning of our relationship that he wasn't attracted to me, because I wasn't "in shape" enough for him. He knew my history. He knew I'd suffered from eating disorders and was sensitive about my weight. I reacted not by dumping him but by moving in with him and dropping ten pounds. I felt the pressure to keep him happy and went to the gym every day. (Fans of *What Not to Wear* might've noticed I went from a size 10 to a size 4 between seasons one and two. Now they know why.) And this guy wasn't the worst type of ex on my list. I've had them all: the guy who made an art out of cheating; the narcissist who couldn't hear a word I said unless we were talking about him; the insecure schmoo who couldn't handle dating a woman who was more successful than he was; the idiot who didn't realize that social media is public unless you change your privacy settings (FYI: Don't flirt with other women online when you are dating someone). My favorite, to date, was the "promance" (trademark pending), an inappropriate liase with someone from a professional setting. I'll just say this: Turns out that on the neurological disorder spectrum, they missed a diagnosis: ASSBURGER.

My point is this: None of these jerks would have made for the best life partner. Nor would men who cowered in the face of my formidable personality. Let's face it, I can be a tough cookie. Not for nothing, I think my laundry list of exes proves my judgment is less than stellar.

Not having been able to maintain a healthy romantic relationship feels like a major fail. I wasn't raised to believe that my marital status would define me. I grew up wanting to feel empowered, successful, and in control of my own destiny. That scenario could certainly include a meaningful relationship. It's not as if I sat myself down and said: Well, it's career or family, guess I'll take career. But I know I couldn't do what I do now professionally, which involves a lot of travel and keeping a hectic schedule, and also be a supportive wife or, further, any kind of parent (except to my cat Baby Al, of course).

As I've said, women can't have it all. What sucks is that we feel like failures if we don't have it all, instead of being proud of what we *do* have. I'm proud and happy that I've based my career on the one thing I can do really well—styling. (I can't cook, garden, hang a picture, sew, paint, sing— although I do that anyway—show tunes, loudly. I can't drive, which is a huge pain in the ass. But if the task at hand involves color, pattern, texture, and shine, I'm your girl.) That one talent has taken me far, and I'm grateful for it. But it would be nice to have the partner along with the cat, the career, and the shoe closet that's bigger than a guest bedroom. (Yeah, that last one is pretty sweet regardless.)

As it stands now, I'm single by choice. Not to say I wouldn't be happy to meet a partner if he's out there (call me! 867-5309). But as far back as I can remember, I thought love was what was going to make me feel whole. And one thing I have learned is that no one can give you that but yourself.

My advice to Annie is this: Be genuine. Concern yourself with whether or not you like the man. If you do, and he likes you back, take it from there. If he doesn't, dust off your hands and say, "Next." There is no point in mooning over someone who doesn't see the greatness of you. I say that from experience. By the time you're forty-something years old—and, in Annie's case, having raised two fabulous kids, been married, divorced, cared for her friends, had a career—she doesn't have a damn thing to prove to anyone.

And when I start to date again, I hope I can take my own advice. But I'll leave the campgrounds to Annie.

Annie's Start-over

THE SYMPTOM:

Black, black, black

THE UNDERLYING CAUSE:

Fear of dating

THE PRESCRIPTION:

Dress like you're available, but not by the hour

Annie mentioned that, when she was married, she dressed to please her husband. Now that she's single and need only please herself, she's at a loss. Single style can certainly be used to attract potential partners. But, more important, it can help women define who they are for themselves.

Dressing with overt sexiness to lure a man? Desperate isn't a good look on anyone. Besides which, in my survey of (straight) male friends, guys think a woman in jeans and a T-shirt is sexier than an overdone designer outfit any day. I don't dress for men. I dress for me. And should a man appreciate the care I put into my outfits, and the confidence I feel wearing them, *bonus*.

Five years postdivorce, Annie's kids are out of the house, and she's finally ready to date again. Understandably, she's a bit shaky. Few scenarios in life are

Tailored, not tight. I think I heard Isaac Mizrahi say that first. Your clothes need to fit and skim your frame but not pull. Don't look like a sausage that's been stuffed into casing.

Love these flirty bags. Just big enough for keys, a lipstick, a credit card, and a twenty or two tens. Something about a great clutch says "lady." It's a good way to add color, pattern, texture, and shine to any outfit and change up a look for evening.

more intimidating than sitting across the table from a stranger and knowing that you're both scrutinizing each other's looks and manner. Is there anything between you—a spark, a connection—but air? The pressure of dating can feel enormous. It's even worse than a job interview, I think, because you're being judged based on someone else's ideal of sexual desirability.

So much of the pressure of dating can be relieved if you know for sure before you walk out the door that you look stylish and attractive according to your own standards, and you don't look like a floozy. With that certainty you can face anyone with confidence. And if he's just not that into you, you can walk way with few regrets, especially if you're wearing good heels. For all the things that don't work between two people, control the things you can and leave the rest up to fate, destiny, whatever.

Should the date go off perfectly, and

you want to remember the blissful night for all time? The mental snapshot will be of you looking sensational, sophisticated, and self-possessed. Much better that than looking like an insecure middle-aged tart.

Annie's greatest fear is that, in calling attention to herself, she'll look needy and, worse, desperate. It is a fine line to walk. As you age it's crucial for your own self-worth to maintain a sense of dignity and control in these situations. The built-in sizing up on both sides of the table can be nerve-racking. If you know you look great—sexy but not trying too hard—you can focus on whether you like him and not worry about what he thinks of you.

If you want to know what I mean, watch Rene Russo in *The Thomas Crown Affair.* That woman did single style in her forties really well.

So, back to the task at hand. How not to dress like you're a desperate slut? Some guidelines:

SHOW A LITTLE SKIN. Flaunting too much skin reads as attention neediness. This is especially true for women over forty. Choose one quadrant to expose. Your chest and arms *or* your back and shoulders *or* your legs.

CLOTHES ARE NOT BOTOX. Wearing a micro-miniskirt does not take ten years off your face. The idea is to look youthful, not

Varying heel heights is important while dating. Be careful going too high for first-date mobility. Have your sky-high stilettos for date three, or five (depending on your rule).

Pay attention to details. Accessories don't only convey personality, they "finish" an outfit. Like a bow on a present, show your date you're the complete package.

young. If you attempt to match a twenty-five-year-old's date outfit, you'll look like a cougar that needs to be put down. No clothes with an odd number (that is juniors sizing). Do not shop with your daughter; do not shop in the same stores; and do not share her clothes.

KEEP IT LOW. Okay, sort of low. I know I can't *believe* I'm saying this: No heels over four inches. You won't be able to move gracefully, for dancing or for an after-dinner stroll. Feeling comfortable in your outfit is just as important as looking stunning in it, especially for a first date.

NO GLITTER MAKEUP. That says "Daddy issues" . . . well, maybe not. At the very least, it's age inappropriate.

SHEER IS TRANSPARENT. Be careful with sheer. If you overdo it, it sends the same message as showing too much skin. As a layering piece, sheer can be beautiful. But if you wear a neon bra underneath a sheer blouse, it better be Mardi Gras or Halloween.

WEAR COLOR. Black = emotional comfort. Color = emotional strength. Yes, black is comfortable and safe. But if you want to date, you can't play it safe and shroud yourself all the time. You need to be seen in order to be seen. Now, there are exceptions, of course. If the black you do wear fits like a glove, shows skin in the right places, and makes you feel like a million bucks, that's a black you can see. (*Ref.* the cover of this book!) An all-black outfit can be associated with a certain aggressive sexual energy as well, something Annie says she wants to avoid, i.e., being perceived as a black widow spider—scary and deadly, and the lady spiders eat their boyfriends. ("She mates, then she kills." Love Debra Winger.) Annie's personality is light and inviting, and her life philosophy is "Live!" They are better represented with at least some color and print.

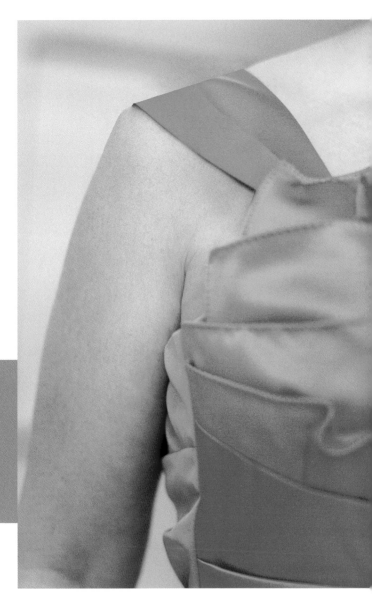

Girly is in the details. Pintucking, ruffles, ruching, pleating, shirring. These kinds of details suggest flirty and feminine without appearing overtly sexy: not many guys walking around with a pintuck. Just an observation.

Why This Works

Despite wearing too much under-the-radar black, Annie loves color and print. That's good, because to get out in the dating world, color and print enable you to be seen.

• **THE DRESS**: She won't just blip on the radar in this. She'll blow it out. Annie loved this dress the minute she put it on. It defines her waist, which is always flattering. She's not used to wearing this much color and print, and she had a real "a-ha!" moment realizing how much she loved it.

• **THE JACKET**: A jacket is always a great completer piece. Because we are showing leg, covering the shoulders and arms prevents flaunting too much skin. Orange is a great contrast for blue eyes. (They are opposites on the color wheel.) While I normally recommend completer pieces in neutrals, this jacket works to complement Annie's eyes and skin and hair colors. Nifty trick: Choose a jacket that's the same color as one in the print of the dress.

• **THE SHOES**: Shoes in nude or a matching skin tone lengthen a bare leg and don't feel as heavy as another neutral (like a black) would. Rather than put Annie in high heels, I opted for a lower, more comfortable height that still flatters her gorgeous gams. The thin heel and peep toe are sexy and feminine and totally age-appropriate.

• **THE JEWELRY**: When in doubt about a necklace *and* earrings, choose one. Too many accessories near the face looks crowded and can cut your neckline, making you look less tall and lean. Try big earrings *or* a necklace with small stud earrings and one other piece of jewelry—bracelets *or* a cocktail ring—on another quadrant of the body.

Here, I mixed colored stones and enamel in colors similar to the ones in Annie's dress with gold to complete the ensemble and help make it look fun, elegant, and expensive overall.

Yes!..............And?

Accept the unvarnished truth and build your style strategy from there.

"I'm forty-eight and single."

Lucky you, getting to start a new chapter when you're young enough to really enjoy it. Your life is only half over, with the wise half remaining. Fortunately, you don't have to compete (*and shouldn't*) with a twenty-eight-year-old in terms of outlook or style. You've lived a rich, full life already. You know you don't need a man to be fulfilled, but it would be nice to have one. You don't have to settle. You know what you like and might as well make a conscious choice to be finicky. The question a twenty-five-year-old asks herself: **Does he like me?** The question a fortysomething asks: **Do I like him?** You honor yourself through style—only the best, truest representation of you will do—and demonstrate how you'd expect a partner to honor and treat you.

"Dating is terrifying."

Even with the wisdom you bring to the game, it **is** scary to put yourself out there. It's also scary to have been married and have kids. Sometimes "scary" is in direct proportion to the potential reward. If you don't scare yourself, you'll stay rooted in the same safe place. That's fine for a lot of women. It's up to the individual how much risk she can tolerate. But if you do want to date, then you have to face the fear, adjust your style, and get the hell out there, Nugget.

"I'm afraid of coming off the wrong way."

The fear is justified. You're meeting new people at a new stage of life. If you're afraid of dressing the wrong way, check yourself before you wreck yourself. What you thought was desirable twenty years ago isn't right for you today. Dressing in a way that purposefully objectifies you, diminishes you. If you give away the slices for free, no one will buy the loaf. You're worth more than that, Baby. If you know the practical rules for dressing appropriately, the fear is vanquished.

"Live!"
Exactly! "Live!" is "yes . . . and" all in one word. Yes, it's what you've been given; and, it's what you can do with it. Annie made a vow to remember the advice of her friend. So take risks, dive in (maybe into a quarry to find an athletic beer drinker?), and try wearing color. I've said before, on many occasions, don't fall back on black. Black can be sophisticated when done correctly. But we also associate it with hiding, mourning, negation, even resignation. All of that runs counter to her newly adopted philosophy.

TEN ITEMS YOU SHOULDN'T HAVE IN YOUR CLOSET THAT WILL REMIND YOU YOU'RE SINGLE

1. Any necklace that has too small a clasp to fasten by yourself.
2. Any bracelet that you need both hands to close the latch.
3. Any top or dress that has French buttons from the neck to the waist.
4. Dresses that have a zipper in the back that requires dislocated shoulders to pull up by yourself.
5. Any complicated clasp on the sleeves that require two hands to fasten.
6. Jeans that are so tight, someone else has to zip them with pliers (not that you have ANY business wearing these in the first place).
7. Any boot so tight on your foot or leg that amputation is the only possible option without another person present.
8. Any clothing with bad associations, e.g., a dress your ex loved that will always remind you of him. Instead, buy a new dress that you love.
9. Your engagement ring. Sell it.
10. A T-shirt that reads "I'm with nobody. But if you see Stupid, tell him to call me."

AND ONE ITEM YOU SHOULD HAVE

A ratty, disgusting pair of pajamas that you wouldn't want anyone to see you in. When your new boyfriend sleeps over (on the third or fifth date, depending on which rule you follow), wear them. If he stays, he's a keeper.

*"If you do not tell the truth about yourself,
you cannot tell it about other people."*

—VIRGINIA WOOLF

ME

Getting Comfy in My Skin

You may or may not know how much I hate the term "comfortable" when it comes to style, but I do. It's like a four letter word to me. Nine times out of ten, when women tell me they are "comfortable" in their outfits—whether sweats or oversize, shapeless, monotone pieces—it's because they feel safe in hiding or ignoring their bodies (willful blindness, so to speak). That kind of comfortable is a rut. It's an excuse to avoid the *un*comfortable (i.e., how you feel about what's underneath all that crap). Many times people who dress badly (avoiding their shape rather than flattering it) do so because they *feel* badly. But embracing personal style can create a different sense of comfort altogether, one that results from harmonizing all that you are on the inside with what you look like on the outside. Fact is, I want you to look good and feel *truly* comfortable all in one package.

In a lot of ways my job at TLC's *What Not to Wear* was tailor-made for me (again, no pun intended). Over the course of my nine seasons on the show, my love of sparkly clothes and high heels has evolved into an understanding of that love and what lies at the heart of it: Style is a form of self-expression and aspiration. Style is there for you to use, to constantly reevaluate: to see yourself differently and to feel differently. It isn't superficial and it is never just about the clothes. Think of it as a "Hello, My Name Is _____" tag, and life as one big convention. It is a tool of opportunity to help demonstrate the *possible*. What I've learned from the show is that style can be a metaphor for other things. It represents how to gain a sense of control. With style, you can see change quickly and feel it viscerally and the belief in your own power translates into other areas of your life. What is magical and mystifying to me about style is not that by seeing we can believe. It is that eventually, we can *believe* because we can see. That is neuroplasticity. We can embrace change the more we can make it tangible.

The ten women in this book (myself included) are all examples of what a shift in perspective can accomplish. Reevaluating our bodies, circumstances, and even the prejudices we held about ourselves led us to a different way to see ourselves.

Proactivity forced us to do and evolve, and my nine ladies left the studio ready to be something new. It is hard to understand that black might be your security blanket unless you try on color. It's hard to see that every age has its own unique beauty if you are still dressing as you did in your youth. It's hard to see the body you actually have if you are wearing clothes four sizes too big. We all have our blind spots—and through style you can learn to see your way clear of them (though that's not to say a whole new bunch won't crop up either).

I have spent a lot of my life re-examining myself and using style as a way to be *more* of who I feel I am. I talk a lot in this book about taking positive control of your image. Part of that control involves embracing change and evolution. That is the whole point of a start-over: At any moment you can evolve to integrate who you are with where you are *right now*, instead of fighting it and holding on to outdated beliefs about yourself. I think what resonated so deeply with me that night at Molly and David's was what the idea of "Yes! . . . And?" really means. It insists on two things that are always available to us: honesty with ourselves and the never-ending ability to improve. The Truth About Style is that it starts with the truth about *you*.

While you may have come to know me because of my style, now you've had a chance to peek behind the proverbial dressing room curtain. While you may have known about my passion for style, now you know the reason that I'm so passionate. It's not an overstatement to say that style teaches me over and over how to live in my skin. It helps me find courage and confidence and control when I feel I have none. While I was drawn to the world of fashion as a little girl because of its sparkle, I love the world of style now because I understand its transformative power.

Style isn't something stagnant. Like us, it's always in flux. It's a valuable exercise to reassess your style, to see if it reflects where you are in your life and not some old notion of who you were. We all strive for that harmony and balance in life, to be who we are. The nine women in this book were ready to see themselves in a new way. By paying attention to their style they allowed for a new focus on who they are *now*. I hope this project reminds them to honor themselves and I hope it reminds you too. It's never about the clothes—it's about what they can *do*.

I don't know whether or not you feel your style is where you want it to be. I'm not judging you. (Okay, I am, quietly. Kidding! . . . Sort of.) What I do know is that understanding yourself, developing your image, and updating your style takes the sting out of anyone *else's* judgment and puts you in the driver's seat. (If, unlike me, you *have* a license.) Isn't that reason enough to try? So, *go. Do. Be.* Get off your tushy and get *dressed*.

As for me, maybe I'm due for a reassessment, too. (Certainly feels that way since starting this book. Not gonna lie. It hasn't been easy to rehash some of this stuff.) Style has taken me places I could never have imagined as an eleven-year-old-girl who could barely stand to look at herself in the mirror. There's more to me now than just wishing to be normal, even more than that style coach you see on TV. Sometimes I wonder if my style is more polished than I actually am. It doesn't always match my goofiness and quirkiness and my very own set of unique flaws. (All right, it doesn't "go." You never want to match.)

Maybe it's time for something a little more . . . relaxed. I may bristle at the word "comfortable" about style, but there is definitely something to the word "comfy." (It's got *five* letters. And it feels . . . dimensional, inclusive of all the different parts of me.)

My "Yes! . . . And?" I want my style to reflect it all: my joy, my struggle, my sparkly, my goofy, my quirky—not some sanitized version of unattainable perfection. Some days I hit just the right note. Some days I don't. But being comfy is being who you are and not opting to hide it.

Maybe a low heel every once in a while wouldn't *kill* me. (Not that I'd get rid of any of the high ones.) And while you won't catch me in sweats anytime soon (or ever, unless you sleep over on the third or fifth date, depending on what rule I am following that day), I am trying to loosen up!

For once, I'll let you be the judge.

Shopping Guide

Here are some lists of designers for you based on the kinds of styles discussed in each chapter of this book. While I don't claim that these are at all comprehensive, they will point you in the right direction should you be interested in any of the subject matter or looks that I've described. These lists run the gamut from mass to high designer, and are meant to be a starting point for your research and to acquaint you with some new brands you may not have heard of. Even if you can't afford some of the suggestions included here, it's a great idea to see what some of today's best designers are doing, both to inspire your own style and to help you spot great items at a lower price point. When it comes to getting dressed, the more information you have, the better your style will be. If I've left any designers off, it's because they didn't fit the categories, I'm just a forgetful schmoo, or I'm not acquainted with them yet. (And if you have other suggestions, I would love for you to let me know so I can add them! Tweet me @stacylondonsays.)

TOUGH AND TENDER

Looking for something with a little bit of attitude?
These designers know how to give it to you.

3.1 Phillip Lim
10 Crosby by
  Derek Lam
A.L.C.
Alexander Wang
Altuzarra

AllSaints Spitalfields
Ann Demeulemeester
Balenciaga
Balmain
BCBGMAXAZRIA
Burning Torch

Clare Tough
Creatures of
    Comfort
Cushnie et Ochs
Cut25
Dallin Chase
Daniel Vosovic
Daryl K.
Elizabeth and James
Gary Graham
Givenchy
H&M
HELMUT LANG
IAN R.N.
IMPROVD

Iro
Isabel Marant
Jen Kao
Karl by Karl
    Lagerfeld
Kevork Kiledjian
Kimberly Ovitz
Madison Marcus
Maje
Malene Birger
Marcus Lupfer
McQ
MM6 Maison Martin
    Margiela
Nellie Partow

Ohne Titel
Opening Ceremony
Pencey
Plastic Island
rag & bone
Rebecca Minkoff
Rick Owens /
    DRKSHDW by
    Rick Owens
Rue du Mail
Sandro
Sessun
Silence & Noise
Stolen Girlfriends
    Club

Theyskens' Theory
Thomas Wylde
Timo Weiland
Topshop
Tribune Standard
Twenty8Twelve
Uniqlo
Vera Wang
VPL
Wes Gordon
Willow
Zadig & Voltaire
Zara
Zero + Maria
    Cornejo

PLUS IS A POSITIVE

The plus market is growing. Here is a list of designers I found who are doing their due diligence and making great plus pieces. Also check online for larger size ranges from some of your favorite sites.

Adrianna Papel
Alfani
Alyx
American Rag
Anne Klein
Calvin Klein
Daisy Fuentes
David Meister
DKNYC
Donna Ricco

East 5th
eloquii by
    The Limited
GAP
H&M+
INC International
    Concepts
J.Crew (online up
    to size 20)
Jessica Howard

Jones New York
Lane Bryant
Lauren by Ralph
    Lauren
Lee Lee's Valise
Liz Claiborne
Madison Plus
Marina Rinaldi
MICHAEL by
    Michael Kors
NYDJ (Not Your
    Daughter's Jeans)

Old Navy
Robbie Bee
Studio 1
Style & Co
Tahari by
    Arthur S. Levine
Talbots
Tahari Women
Worthington

SOFT SERVE

Whether you are recovering from illness or just want to be comfy, these designers are doing it with supreme style.

American Apparel	Feel the Piece	Madewell	T by Alexander
American Vintage	Gap	Malo	Wang
Autumn Cashmere	Heather	M. Patmos	Target
C&C California	Henry Lehr	Qi	T-bags Los Angeles
Chinti & Parker	Inhabit	Quincy	Three Dots
Claudia Schiffer	James Perse	Rachel Pally	Torn by Ronny
Clu	Jardin des Oranges	Rick Owens Lilies	Kobo
Crumpet	J.Crew	Saint Grace	Uniqlo
Dear Cashmere	Kain	Seaton	Velvet by Graham
Duffy	Lanston	Sunny Leigh	& Spencer
Ella Moss	Lutz & Patmos	Splendid	White & Warren

PETITE FLOWER

Not all these designers have separate petite lines but they cut small enough to accommodate petites in many cases. Always check online to see if your fave designers make petites, which they may only offer on their site.

Acne	A.P.C.
Addison	Banana Republic
alice + olivia	Boy. By Band of
Ann Taylor	Outsiders / girl. by
Aritzia	Band of Outsiders

Calvin Klein
Charlotte Ronson
Dolce Vita
Gryphon
Isabel Marant /
    Etoile by Isabel
    Marant
INC International
    Concepts
J.Crew

Jen Kao
Lover
Mara Hoffman
Miu Miu
McQ Alexander
    McQueen
Oak / A.OK
Opening Ceremony
Parker
Rachel Antonoff

River Island
Rory Beca
sass & bide
Sea
See By Chloe
Simply Vera
    Vera Wang
Steven Alan
Style&co.
Topshop

Urban Outfitters
Athe Vanessa Bruno
Victoria Beckham
Versus by Versace
Zara
Zimmerman

M.O.M.
MASTERS OF MULTITASKING

Moms can shop from any of these lists but for convenience, price point, and ease, I listed these designers as some go-to choices. (Also see Soft Serve)

Gryphon
Joe Fresh
Kai-aakmann
L'Agence
Le Mont St
    Michel
LOFT
Madewell
New York &
    Company
Nili Lotan
Old Navy

ORGANIC by
    John Patrick
Rogan
Rory Beca
Spring & Clifton
Steven Alan
Target
Theory
Tommy Hilfiger
Uniqlo
Veda
Vince

Ann Taylor
Aritzia
Aubin & Wills
ba&sh
Boden
Brochu Walker

Closed
ck Calvin Klein
Club Monaco
Ellen Tracy
Express
Gap

POWER DRESSING

Sculptural, architectural, tailored, and appropriate for any age .

Alexander McQueen	Dolce&Gabbana		
Alaïa	Equipment		
Akris	Haider Ackermann	Neil Barret	Rochas
Araks	HELMUT LANG	New York &	Smythe
Ann Taylor	Hermes	Company	Stella McCartney
Banana Republic	HUGO BOSS	Oscar de la Renta	Tahari
Band of Outsiders	J.Crew	Paul Smith	Talbots
Bibhu Mohapatra	Jenni Kayne	Peter Som	Ted Baker
Billy Reid	JIL SANDER	Piazza Sempione	Theory
Bottega Veneta	Joseph	Pink Tartan	Tom Ford
Burberry	Lyn Devon	PORTS 1961	The Row
Calvin Klein	Maiyet	Prabal Gurung	Victoria Beckham
CÉLINE	Martin Grant	PRADA	Victor & Rolf
Chaiken & Capone	Max Mara	Rachel Roy	Yves Saint Laurent
by Chaiken	Michael Kors	Rachel Zoe	
Chloe	Naeem Khan	Reed Krakoff	
Derek Lam	Narciso Rodriguez	Richard Nicoll	

VERTICALLY BLESSED

Brands that cater to Glamazons. Again, always check online to see if some of your fave designers offer tall size ranges on their websites.

Ann Taylor	DKNY
Banana Republic	Gap
Chaiken & Capone	J.Crew
by Chaiken	

Lafayette 148
   New York
LOFT
Lucky Brand

Max Mara
MICHAEL by
   Michael Kors
New York and Company

Old Navy
PHILOSOPHY
   di Alberta Ferretti
Talbots

Topshop
Tory Burch

LIVE OUT LOUD

If you are after color and print. all these designers make beautiful statements.

12th Street by
   Cynthia Vincent
Alice & Trixie
Anna Sui
Anthropologie
Ashish
Cacharel
Carven
Chelsea Flower
Christian Cota
Clements Ribeiro
Clover Canyon
Corey Lynn Calter
Creatures of the
   Wild
Cynthia Rowley
Cynthia Steffe

Dries Van Noten
Duro Olowu
Diane von
   Furstenberg
Easton Pearson
Erdem
Etro
Free People
Gap
Gar—de
Gregory Parkinson
Henry Holland
ICB
Issa
J.Crew
Jenni Kayne
Jill Stuart

Joe Fresh
Jonathan Saunders
Joie
Karen Walker
kate spade
Kenzo
L.A.M.B.
Lem Lem
Libertine
Marc Jacobs / Marc
   by Marc Jacobs
Mason
Matthew
   Williamson
Mary Katrantzou
Marni
Milly
Miu Miu
Nanette Lepore/
   Oonagh by
   Nanette Lepore
Patterson J.
   Kincaid
Paul & Joe

Peter Pilotto
PRADA
Preen / Preen Line
Proenza Schouler
Rachel Comey
Rebecca Taylor
Roksanda Ilincic
ROZAE R.N.
Sachin + Babi
Sonia Rykiel /
   Sonia by Sonia
   Rykiel
Suno
TEXTILE Elizabeth
   and James
Thakoon
Tibi
Tracy Reese
Trina Turk
Tusmori Chisato
Tucker
Walter
Winter Kate
Yumi Kim

GET YOUR FLIRT ON

Cannot go wrong with a gorgeous date dress.
Just saying.

ABS Allen Schwartz
Alexis Mabille
alice + olivia
Alessandra Rich
Azzaro
Badgley Mischka
Bebe
Black Halo
Carmen Marc Valvo
camilla and marc
CÉLINE
CHANEL
David Meister
Dolce&Gabbana
doo.Ri
Erin Fetherston

Gucci
Hakaan
Halston Heritage
Herve Leger by Max Azria
Honor by Giovanna Randall
ISSA
Jason Wu
Jay Godfrey
Jill Stuart
Kay Unger
LANVIN
Lela Rose
L'Wren Scott
Laundry by Shelli Segal

La Petite Salope
Maggy London
Marchesa
Max & Chloe
Miguelina
BCBGMAXAZRIA
Naeem Khan
Narciso Rodriguez
Nicole Miller
Nina Ricci
Phoebe Couture
Preen
Rachel Roy
Reiss
Riller & Fount
Robert Rodriguez
Roksanda Ilincic

Roland Mouret
Rolando Santana
Shoshanna
Sophie Theallet
TADASHI SHOJI
Thread
Tracy Reese / Plenty by Tracy Reese
Valentino
Victoria Beckham
White House Black Market
Yigal Azrouel
Zac Posen / Z Spoke Zac Posen

SHOES

Does not include designers who make
clothing as well. These peeps really do shoes.

80%20
ALDO
Alexandre Birman
Ash
Bernardo

Brian Atwood / B by Brian Atwood
Burak Uyan
Camilla Skovgaard
Casadei

Charlotte Olympia
Christian
  Louboutin
Chrissy Morris
Cole Haan
Dolce Vita / DV
  Dolce Vita (Ok I
  lied. They have
  clothes too)
Fiorentini + Baker
Frye

George Esquivel
Giuseppe Zanotti
Jean-Michel Cazabat
Jessica Simpson
  (she does too)
Jimmy Choo
K. Jacques
Kathryn Amberleigh
LD Tuttle
Loeffler Randall
Manolo Blahnik

Matt Bernson
MIA
Modern Vintage
Nicholas Kirkwood
Nine West /
  Boutique 9
Pedro García
Pour La Victoire
Pura López
Repetto
Sam Edelman

Sergio Rossi
Seychelles
Sigerson Morrison /
  belle by Sigerson
  Morrison
Steven by Steve
  Madden / Steve
  Madden
Stuart Weitzman
Tabitha Simmons
Walter Steiger

DENIM

Just some of my fave denim designers.
Does *not* include designers who do denim
in their lines unless denim is their main
thing.

7 for All Mankind
A.P.C.
AG
Basic Editions
BDG
Black Orchid
BLANKNYC
BLK DNM
Canyon River

Cheap Monday
Citizens of
  Humanity
Current/Elliott
Denizen
Diesel
DKNY Jeans
DL1961 Premium
  Denim

Dylan George
Earnest Sewn
Faded Glory
Gap
Genetic Denim
Goldsign
Habitual
Henry & Belle
HELMUT LANG
Hudson
James Jeans
J Brand
J.Crew
JOE'S Jeans
Lee

Levi's Made and
  Crafted
Madewell
MiH
Miss Tina
Mother
Notify
NYDJ (Not Your
  Daughter's Jeans)
Nudie Jeans
Old Navy
Paige Denim
Prps
R13
rag & bone/JEAN

Raven Denim	ROCK & REPUBLIC	Siwy	Superfine
Red Rivet	Route 66	SOLD Design Lab	Tiger of Sweden
Rich & Skinny	Signature by	Sofia by	Uniqlo
Riders by Lee	Levi Strauss & Co	Sofia Vergara	Won Hundred

RESOURCES

Use your department stores' online sites for shopping, trends, strategy, and inspiration!

Amazon.com	Last Call
ASOS.com	Loehmann's
Barneys New York	Lord & Taylor
Belk	Luisaviaroma.com
Bergdorf Goodman	Macy's
Bloomingdale's	Marshalls
Century 21	mytheresa.com
Dillard's	Neiman Marcus
Fashism.com	NET-A-PORTER.com
Filene's Basement	Nordstrom
forwardforward.com	Nordstrom Rack
Gilt.com	Polyvore.com
JCPenney	Saks Fifth Avenue
Kmart	OFF 5TH
Kohl's	THEOUTNET.com
LaGarconne.com	Saks Fifth Avenue

Sears	Target
Shopstyle.com	T.J.Maxx
Style.com	Walmart
StyleCaster.com	YOOX.com
StyleforHire.com*	Zappos.com

DISCLAIMER: *This is my company. When you are ready for some face-to-face style assistance and budget strategy, my stylists are amazeballs. I guarantee it.*

Gratitude

I'd like to thank the following for their invaluable contribution to this book:

To Valerie Frankel: Without you, this book would, literally, not have been written. Thanks for your brilliance, parking skills, and weekly visits.

To Chadwick Tyler: For his beautiful vision and skill, his awesome family, and his ability to capture the essence of each model, myself included. You are the humbling ground, my friend.

To my models—Annie, Ashley, Janise, June, Sarah C., Sarah M., Tania, Tracy, Ty: For sharing your stories, for being so beautiful inside and out, and your amazing enthusiasm to see yourselves in a new way.

To Laura Nespola: For being the world's best producer, most diplomatic e-mailer (you should win a Nobel Peace Prize) and for reviving my love of a sticker.

To Rick Kot: For being hands-down the coolest editor in the biz, and the one with the keenest insight for the necessity (or non-necessity) of curse words, bourbon, and macarons.

To Clare Ferraro: You got me from the word "lipstick." Thanks for believing in this project.

To Carolyn Coleburn: For getting the word out.

To the art directors Roseanne Serra and Amy Hill: I don't know what to say but thank you. A special shout-out to Amy for the brilliant insight "Just don't call it an introduction."

To my designer, Renato Stanisic: For his incredible talent, dedication, superhuman speed, and endless empathy.

To my stylists—Matthew Simoneli, Zoë Sundra, Keia Bounds, and Emily Eisen— whose talent is reflected in every photo: Thank you for inspiring me.

To all the designers and showrooms: For graciously sending merchandise.

To Kasey Madgett: For being my assistant . . . which doesn't even begin to sum up all she has to put up with. And for intuiting a good time for green juice and a good time for chocolate.

To Casey R. Anderson: For his beautiful filmmaking and empathy for the project.

To Robert Dume: For his amazing time-lapse video and speeding up what felt like an endless process.

To Shawn Bell: For making sure we had sound. It'd be tough if you couldn't hear us.

To hair and makeup: Sarah Tanno (makeup), Charley Brown (hair), Mathew Nigara (makeup) for working their magic on my "raw material." To Samatha Trinh (makeup) and Michael Dueñas (hair) for enhancing the natural beauty of my models. To Julie Kandalec for the coolest mani-pedis ever.

To the photo assistant Delilah Jesinkey (aka Selina Kyle): Your secret's safe with me. To Skyler Smith: For sitting on an old lady's lap.

To my stylists' assistants—Daniel Edley, Fhonia Ellis, Kathryn Mclain, Kimberly Barker, Lauren Matina: For their hard work, positive attitude, and awesome ability to run.

To the hair and makeup assistants Walter Nunez and Dominique Farina: For their kickass backup support and attention to detail.

To the style interns—Allison Cirbus, Antonia Riley, Christopher Lee, Jessica Bindrim, Kamala Randjecovic, Kristi Turner, Penny Chiu, Rachel Gittler: For taking the time to pitch in and help whenever necessary without hesitation.

To the production team Brendan Bock and Jessica Miglio: For supplying the grease that makes this whole dirty business run (yes, moviephiles, I *am* quoting *Mommie Dearest*) and for returning all of my furniture in one piece (not that we used any of it).

To Anna Fagin (casting): For her countless hours sorting through our models submissions, awesome spreadsheets, and one-pagers.

To Maria Rizzo at Halcyon Gourmet: For the best food ever. Period.

To Monte Engler and Helene Freeman at Phillips Nizer: For dealing in legalese, a language I will, thankfully, never understand.

To Simon Green and Lisa Shotland at CAA: You guys wanted me to write a book, remember? Thanks for seeing me through it.

To TLC: For the opportunity of a lifetime.

To Jack Studios: For the Ping-Pong table and the Nest grapefruit candle. Big shout-out to Leila, who thinks she rocks a better gray streak than I do.

To Industria Superstudio: For their patience and super-cool brick wall used for our impromptu photo shoot after the photo shoot.

To my family: For not leaving me on a doorstep, though this thought may have occurred to you more than once. Mom, Poppyrazzi, Vickirazzi, Swizzles, and Sizzles: I love you more than I could ever say. D.: YOU ARE THE BEST COPY EDITOR IN THE WHOLE UNIVERSE.

To Baby Al, who will have to have this read aloud to him as he never learned to read: Thank you for the nightly face bath, always a good way to get off the makeup, and for loving snuggles as much as I do.

To the cast of *Glee*: For doing the best version of "Teenage Dream" ever. I salute you. Rock on.

To the cast of *Book of Mormon*: One word: Hello.

Photo Credits

by Riki Rosetta; scarves by eloquii by The Limited

Page 113: dress by Lee Lee's Valise

Page 115: blazer by eloquii by The Limited; blouse by Calvin Klein; skirt by IGIGI by Yuliya Raquel; shoes by Marc Fisher; belt by Lee Lee's Valise; earrings from Sorelli; ring by Lee Angel; bracelet by Alexis Bittar

JUNE

Page 129: coat by Tucker

Page 130: shoes by L.K. Bennett

Page 131: tank by Reiss

Page 131: jacket by Hugo Boss; blouse by Jones New York; trouser by Adam Lippes

Page 133: suit by Elie Tahari; blouse by Hugo Boss; shoes by Reiss; earrings by

Kimberly McDonald; necklace by Gerard Yosca; hematite stretch bracelet by Kenneth Jay Lane; uvaronite garnet and diamond ring by Kimberly McDonald; crystal gold ring by Lee Angel

SARAH M.

Page 147: top by Lafayette 148

Page 148: pants by Lafayette 148; shoes by Ann Taylor

Page 149: blouse by Lafayette 148; skirt by Ann Taylor

Page 150: jewelry by Jessica Robinson, Simon Tu, Lee Angel, Gerard Yosca, RJ Graziano, & Sorrelli

Page 151: top by Lafayette 148; skirt by Ann Taylor

Page 153: cardigan by Lane Bryant; blouse by Lafayette 148; jeans by Lafayette 148; shoes by Ann

Taylor; cuff by Alexis Bittar; earrings by New York & Co.

TRACY

Page 167: jacket by Zara TRF; scarf by eloquii by The Limited

Page 168: blouse by Tucker

Page 168: blouse by Yumi Kim

Page 169: blouse by Yumi Kim; jeans by Banana Republic; shoes by Coclico

Page 170: jacket by BCBG; blouse by Cynthia Steffe; jeans by Banana Republic

Page 171: blouse by Tucker; jacket by Zara TRF; jeans by Banana Republic

Page 173: cardigan by J.Crew; blouse by Tucker; skirt by Rachel Roy; shoes by Marc Fisher; belt by eloquii by The Limited; clutch by M. Clifford; ring by

Sorelli; brooch by Alexis Bittar

ANNIE

Page 187: dress by Reiss

Page 188: clutches by Melie Bianco, Santi, MC Clifford, and Pono by Joan Goodman

Page 189: shoes (left to right): Calvin Klein, Stuart Weitzman, Stuart Weitzman

Page 190: dress by Reiss; necklace by Gerard Yosca

Page 191: dress by Ports 1961

Page 193: dress by Kay Unger; shoes by Michael Kors; earrings and bangles by Wendy Mink; bracelet by Gerard Yosca; ring by Kenneth Jay Lang

Foundational garments by Natori, Commando, Cosabella, and Spanx.

Photos of Stacy